ACCOUNTING WITH HEART

CHINA'S ROLE IN INTERNATIONAL FINANCE AND BUSINESS

ACCOUNTING WITH HEART

CHINA'S ROLE IN INTERNATIONAL FINANCE AND BUSINESS

WANG JUN

WILEY

John Wiley & Sons (Asia) Pte. Ltd.

Copyright © 2010 John Wiley & Sons (Asia) Pte. Ltd.
Published in 2010 by John Wiley & Sons (Asia) Pte. Ltd.
2 Clementi Loop, #02-01, Singapore 129809

Other Wiley Editorial Offices
John Wiley & Sons, 111 River Street, Hoboken, NJ 07030, USA
John Wiley & Sons, The Atrium, Southern Gate, Chichester, West Sussex, P019 8SQ,
    United Kingdom
John Wiley & Sons (Canada) Ltd., 5353 Dundas Street West, Suite 400, Toronto, Ontario,
    M9B 6HB, Canada
John Wiley & Sons Australia Ltd, 42 McDougall Street, Milton, Queensland 4064,
    Australia
Wiley-VCH, Boschstrasse 12, D-69469 Weinheim, Germany

Library of Congress Cataloging-in-Publication Data
ISBN 978-0-470-82570-9

Typeset in 10.5/13pt Sabon-Roman by Thomson Digital
Printed in Hong Kong by Printplus Limited
10 9 8 7 6 5 4 3 2 1

CONTENTS

FOREWORD

On behalf of the Association of Chartered Certified Accountants (ACCA), I am delighted to congratulate Dr. Wang Jun on his first international publication, whose inspiring writings deserve a wider audience.

As Vice Minister of Finance, Wang Jun has played an historic part in the development of the Chinese accountancy profession. In 1988, he took a leading role in the creation of the Chinese Institute of Certified Public Accountants (CICPA), marking the beginning of a new era for the nation's profession. Since then, through promoting convergence between Chinese and international accounting standards, Wang Jun has enabled the accountancy profession in China to take its rightful place on the global stage. By advocating the importance of sharing a common understanding of accounting language and principles, he has made a profound contribution to China's international standing and the success and stability of its economy.

In 2008, ACCA was honored to pay tribute to two decades of remarkable achievement by CICPA and pledge its continued support for the Chinese profession, the Ministry of Finance and influential leaders such as Wang Jun under the theme of *Partners in Progress*. To coincide with the publication of this volume, ACCA is recognizing Wang Jun's personal contribution to this effort with a unique "Outstanding Innovation and Leadership Award."

A thinker as well as a man of action, Wang Jun is rightly celebrated across China for the range of his vision and the poetry of his words.

In the western world, the examination of business and finance can often be a dry exercise. Wang Jun shows, through this extraordinary collection of writings, both the breadth of his world view and the connections which surely exist between finance, the arts, spirituality and culture. His is a visionary voice, which takes the reader beyond the normal realm of finance discourse.

As the global economy develops, new models for growth and economic sustainability have emerged. China's astonishing success is an outstanding example of what is a new world order. In understanding the contribution that China's accounting profession has made to its extraordinary economic progress, Wan Jun's writings are a fascinating place to begin.

Helen Brand
Chief Executive
Association of Chartered Certified Accountants

Wang Jun, in his role as China's Vice Minister of Finance in recent years and as Secretary-General of the China Accounting Standards Committee, has been at the center of his country's remarkable advances in financial reporting and accounting.

It has been my pleasure, as Chairman of the International Accounting Standards Board (IASB), to get to know Wang Jun both personally and professionally.

Serious contacts between our two organizations began over four years ago. By that time China had already embarked on a path towards convergence of its own accounting standards for business enterprises and the IASB's International Financial Reporting Standards (IFRSs). In the previous year China had published exposure drafts of a general basic standard and 20 specific standards and had begun a review of its existing 16 standards. A series of meetings between IASB staff and the Ministry of Finance was followed by a high level meeting in Beijing, co-chaired by Wang Jun and myself, in November 2005. The meeting was attended by leading Chinese officials and by three other IASB members and two IASB directors. At the meeting the IASB team applauded and expressed our sincere admiration for the enormous progress already made towards convergence, and agreed to assist China in its work on convergence. For its part China agreed to assist the IASB in researching and developing recommendations on a number of accounting issues that were of particular relevance to that country's unique circumstances and environment.

I am happy to record that since that meeting the IASB has continued to strengthen its ties with China and to move forward in a spirit of cooperation with the Chinese accounting community.

As Wang Jun appreciates very well, accounting standards are only one of the essential elements in establishing a modern economy within the global marketplace. Standards will have no effect unless they have the support and understanding of a well-trained accounting profession, inspired by the highest professional ideals and skills and able to ensure that standards are applied thoroughly and consistently. I have observed with admiration the energy and determination with which the Ministry of Finance, under Wang Jun's wise leadership, has promoted the development of such a cadre of professionals.

If China, rapidly becoming one of the world's leading economies, is now equipped with the accounting tools and skills to take its rightful place on the global business stage, it is largely a tribute to the vision and leadership of my colleague Wang Jun. I am delighted that the publication of this book will enable an international audience to hear him speak for himself.

David Tweedie
Chairman
International Accounting Standards Board

INTRODUCTION

In recent years, the Chinese accountancy profession has experienced an unprecedented period of great growth, change and development as it serves better the requirements of an era of reform and opening up. An old Chinese saying, "The way to govern is through winning people over," speaks of the urgent need to build accounting talent that is globally-minded, has a firm grip on the law, and is innovative, in order to promote the cause of China's accounting reform and development strongly and continually.

This book is a collection of some of my research on the issue of training senior talent in the Chinese accountancy profession. It outlines my thoughts on this issue and on the promotion of the development of the Chinese accountancy profession. I hope that it will reveal a small part of the colorful development of China's economy and accountancy profession, and that it will connect with readers, drawing resonance, reflection and inspiration.

My gratitude extends to everyone who cares about China and the accountancy profession!

Wang Jun
November 6, 2009

Chapter 1

Recharging Yourself to Face the Challenge[1]

I am very happy to have the opportunity today to talk about the issues facing on-the-job[2] graduate students. I'd like to begin not by talking about any particular major principle but by sharing with you my own experience as a working graduate student and the result of my studies, in the hope that this may serve to inspire and help you.

In preparing for this occasion, I wrote down an initial draft of my speech and showed it to my daughter, a third-year student at Peking University, to get her opinion. Before she read it, and not appreciating the decades of history between me and this school, she was a little skeptical that I should have anything to say. After reading the draft, however, she had changed her mind and was, in fact, a little upset that she felt unable to express herself as well. "Even when I do have some overwhelming feelings, why can I not write them down on paper like this?" she asked.

I thought about this for a minute before replying, "Because happy things happen to you one after another when you are at such a young age; you have so much happiness that you become inured to it. Also, your pen and your soul have not yet worked together long enough to create a good fit; only those who have experienced hardship are able to make them fit well. You are still in school, so of course you have not had the chance to experience different lifestyles and realize the sweetness of student life by comparison. You can see how cozy school is only when you have left it; and you only realize more profoundly the enormous role that school has in shaping people's minds if you return to campus after having been out there in society."

She did not really say anything in response, and just kept nodding her head. It seemed like she had understood what I said, but at the same time had not fully understood it. Indeed, I'm not sure that anyone can fully understand what it's like unless they have experienced it for themselves.

PEKING UNIVERSITY: A DREAM SHARED BY FATHER AND DAUGHTER

I have been privileged to live in a time of unique opportunities. My youth was a period of great expectations yet extreme confusion, and Peking University was a dream I held close throughout this time. When I was a child, her name echoed in my ears. During the "Down to The Countryside" movement,[3] I was given the post of team leader of a production crew. At that time, although I willingly accepted re-education through agricultural learning and made great efforts to understand the poor peasants with whom I worked, I also dreamed of one day being a student of Peking University. During the day, I would labor ardously and then in the evenings I would read tirelessly by the light of an oil lamp. I read popular books of the time such as the *Selected Works of Mao Zedong*, the *History of Entrepreneurship*, *How the Steel was Tempered* and *The Gadfly*, and I also tried every way I could to get hold of books on history and politics.

After the re-establishment of college entrance examinations, I was more determined than ever to work hard in my studies and my aim was to study law or politics at Peking University. When filling out my preference for college admission in 1977, I put down just one name, that of Peking University. Disappointingly, I flunked the entrance exam and failed to be admitted. In 1978, after six months of further revision, believing in my heart that the honor of attending Peking University was reserved for those rare few with exceptional intelligence and not for an ordinary person like me, I applied for a place in Zhongnan University of Finance and Economics and was admitted. At that time, there were many great teachers at Zhongnan and, longing for education, I benefited greatly from what the school had to offer. However, despite all this, I still felt a sense of loss that I had been unable to get the grades necessary to fulfill my dream; it became a major regret that I held in the bottom of my heart for a long time. After graduating from Zhongnan in 1982, I took a position with the State and spent the next 20 years there. Over that time there were opportunities to apply to Peking University as a graduate student, but I missed out on them all: my workload and my frequent transfers to different posts combined to make my dream more remote than ever.

The turning point came thanks to my daughter. When she was still at junior high school we started to make plans for her future university education. I suggested to her that she view the campuses of all the major universities in and outside the capital, so that she could get a real feel for higher education establishments and become better informed in making her choice. The first school on the schedule was Peking University. Once there, my daughter was immediately swept away by the scenic views of the Yan Gardens and deeply inspired by the refined atmosphere of learning. From pure excitement, we forgot ourselves and, unexpectedly, spent all day there. Before leaving the campus she declared, "I am going to apply for admission to this university; we do not need to go and see any of the others!" In 2000, my daughter was in Year 1 of high school and really aware of the building pressure. But she never chose to quit. Perhaps it was because she wanted me to help share some of her burden, or perhaps it was to fulfill a dream that she knew I shared, that she suggested in all earnestness that I apply for a doctoral program at the University and that this would be a prerequisite for her own application to the school. Doing it for her and for myself, I clenched my teeth and agreed; my long buried dream returned to my heart.

After this, I started a grueling five months of preparation for the entrance examinations to compete with men and women more than 10 years younger. I would never have thought it before, but in this arena I found undiscovered energy and unlocked previously hidden potential.

At 6.30 PM one Friday in May 2000, after attending a Party Committee Meeting of my organization, I rushed to Peking University's Ziyuan Guest House to prepare for the entrance examinations, which began the following day. That night, I was up revising until two in the morning. I took a total of seven examinations between the Saturday and the following Tuesday. On Tuesday lunchtime I returned home, where my daughter had prepared the most delicious food for me. Faced with her respect and encouragement, my anxiety and fatigue after all those examinations completely dissipated.

People say that you cannot study when you are over 40. When I received my letter of acceptance into the doctoral program of the College of Government Administration of Peking University, I had already turned 41.

September 6, 2000 was, I remember, a cool, refreshing autumn day and the sun was shining gloriously. Accompanied by my daughter, I intentionally entered Peking University from the stately West Gate. Walking through the campus past the inscribed door plates, the heroic lion sculptures, the marble pillars and the tall cedars, I had the feeling of being transported away, as if I was walking inside a beautiful painting. My path of missed opportunities, fortunate circumstances, bitter lessons and the reliving of joy all seemed to become distilled into a higher level of existence in the warmth and calm of the campus. My first profound sentiment as a student of the University was this: It is not that Peking University is a goal too high to attain; it is that our personal growth is limited by our mindset. What people are lacking is not an innate intellect and opportunities in life, but dreams and the perseverance to pursue them. People lack the awareness to admit their own failure and the courage to take a second chance. "If you can take in different concepts, there is no idea that you cannot appreciate; if you can arouse your ambition, there is nothing that you cannot achieve!"[4]

Even more fortunate, and something in which I take even more pride, is the fact that in 2002 my daughter was also admitted to the University through the high school examinations. The opportunity for father and daughter to be studying at the same school at the same time is certainly a wish rarely fulfilled! Whenever I think of this, I cannot help smiling. To be honest, I haven't stopped smiling since the day my daughter was admitted.

MOLDING AND CREATING: "THE COMPANY OF VIRTUOUS PERSONS ENHANCES THE INTELLECT"

If getting into Peking University was the result of my hard work, the spirit of challenging myself that was forged during my studies there was to be an unexpected and treasured gift of personal wealth, and something even more meaningful than the admission itself. I often regard those four years of studying as the Cambrian Period of my life. Just as in that crucial period changes in the external environment hastened evolution and a massive explosion of species, similarly the University's atmosphere, environment, customs and traditions provided the scope for a gathering of minds, clashes, fission and sublimation into unlimited possibilities for students hungry for knowledge.

Universities exist not just to gather young people who are quick in seeking knowledge and courageous in exploration, or more senior people with an encyclopedic knowledge, experience and a discerning approach to conduct research. Rather, their raison d'être is to maintain the connection between knowledge and real life in an active and energetic environment that can nurture imaginative thinking and innovation. Research, absorption and creation all call for intelligence, clear minds, heartfelt compassion, magnanimity, courage and dedication. Universities exist for these reasons and that is why these institutions have always played such a significant role in the evolution of human civilization. Peking University has played a strong role in promoting modernization and progress in China's modern history because of the uniform direction shared by her education philosophy, administrative approach, University spirit and cultural atmosphere. Professor Xie Mian of the University's Chinese Department once said something that, to me, captures the essence of the University:

> This really is a sacred place. For decades, several generations of China's most excellent scholars have been nurtured here. Profound knowledge, brilliant wisdom and tireless and lofty, independent thought—all of this combines with conscientious and careful thinking, magnificent and upright character and integrity and a courageous fighting spirit. Surely such charisma is a spiritual synthesis.

After working for many years and then looking back to reflect on those words, I appreciate even more deeply the value of such perseverance, the importance of independent thought and how everlasting passions and loyalty can motivate progress in our work.

During my time at Peking University, I learned about the unique spirit and atmosphere of independent thought and liberal development. In 1919, the then president of the University, Fu Sinian, urged: "Do away with inherited scientific thought and introduce modern-age scientific thought; do away with subjective arbitrary thought and introduce objective skepticism; work for the future of society and not for the society of today." Zhang Zhongxing, an alumnus of Peking University, remembers: "Once inside the doors of Peking University there were intangible and unwritten supreme rules in governance; this is called an air for learning. One calls it an ambiance, because it has no sound or smell, but in fact it is very powerful."[5] The power of ambiance is not of enforcement but, rather, of potential awe. Insight, imagination, the ability to make judgments and the ability to appreciate, which a university student must possess, can only be nurtured in an atmosphere full of reason and sensitivity. Free of constraint, soaked in calm and ease, universities have their own landscape that has been there forever. After years of working, it was impossible that my thoughts had not become set in their ways or boxed in. Entering university at this point, I could feel all of these rigid constraints gradually melting away. It was like re-experiencing the energy of a fresh spring shower.

While studying at Peking University, I kept in my heart the upright and incorruptible character of my excellent professors, their experience in witnessing great changes in the world, their vast, encyclopedic knowledge and their conscientiousness and perseverance towards learning and teaching. The scientific methodology and the extensive knowledge of my tutor, Professor Wang Puqu, left a huge influence on me. I particularly remember his words: "The company of virtuous persons enhances one's intellect." Professor Wang gave me a great deal of guidance and advice with regard to the writing of my doctoral thesis and with respect to my work for the State, from which I greatly benefited. As for the other teachers, some brought new and interesting material to their subjects, enlivening the atmosphere; they were easy to approach and were highly motivational. Others presented original views and made complex theories more comprehensible. Some spoke with assurance, offering extensive citations, often accompanied by warm laughter, allowing us to gain more life experience in a relaxed and pleasant manner. Like a flame passing from branch to branch as it consumes the fuel, the words and actions of our teachers clearly expressed that the ideals and mission of universities do not simply relate to the nurturing of a group of intellectuals with diplomas: They are more about the passing of the torch of thought and convictions, a remolding and a spreading of a spirit, creating a kind of ambience that can enrich personal character, eliminate materialistic desire and enhance moral status.

What was memorable for me during this period was the clash and interaction of minds between students and how we expanded our horizons. Students "were able to encourage themselves with their own moral integrity"[6] and place integrity above professional success. I benefited greatly from my interactions and communication with them. Henry Rosovsky, former Dean of the Faculty of Arts and Sciences at Harvard University, once said, "At Harvard, I often hear people say students can learn more by learning from each other than they can directly from teachers . . . I see it as praise for a meticulously selected student population of great diversity and exceptional talent."[7] Like Harvard, Peking University has always attracted and gathered a student population with a fervent sense of mission and duty and countless people with noble aspirations to explore the truth about saving their country and people.

Confucius said: "In a group of three people, there is always something to learn" and on-the-job students, bathed in their social experiences, can be a treasure to their fellow students. Not only can they draw on each other's business experiences, they can also enter into discussions about personal qualities and work styles. For example, Gao Pengcheng was a student at Peking University from his undergraduate days all the way through to his doctoral studies. This enabled him to see all problems from a theoretical angle and systematically elaborate on issues based on the principles of his academic knowledge. There were things that we could not describe or explain even at great length, but he could sum them up with just a single notion; sometimes he would make a situation instantly clear to us all by a theoretical explanation. Of course, he was also able to learn many examples and material from the real world from me and other on-the-job students and constantly enrich his own theoretical research.

The biggest reward, though, was learning the responsibility and passion to serve the country and its citizens. I worked diligently to confront my inner self; absorb new experiences and continually enrich myself; to embrace my work post and respect the profession and to carry out my duties to the best of my ability. As a civil servant, I understand that the duties I undertake relate to the image of the government, the reputation of the political power and the support of the masses. I strive to speak well and act with discretion in my work, to comply diligently with the administration and to perform my duties respectfully and with commitment. I focused more clearly on the better management of public finance through considering policies from a financial perspective and analyzing and determining matters of financial policy through practising the important philosophy laid out by the "Three Represents"[8] and implementing the "scientific concept of development."[9] For this reason, I chose as the subject of my doctoral dissertation "The construction and expansion of the public finance sector in China's transformation period" in order to research the topic of finance as fully as possible within the context of public administration and political science.

I learned to consider China within the framework of an international structure. If we do not contemplate issues from an international perspective, and only perceive them with patriotic sentiment, I am afraid we will not bring about good results, and this may even lead to mistakes for the country. Over several years I have had the opportunity to make research trips to a number of countries, including the Philippines, South Africa, Egypt and Hungary, and have published a series of articles based on my studies.[10]

By continuously expanding my horizons and by repeatedly undertaking comparative research, I have been able to maintain my passion in studying and struggling for my country and this ensures that my work and my studies continue to grow and benefit each other.

For example, in 2003, when China was working to resolve the issue of export tax rebates, the tax rebate rate of certain IT products was reduced. Some IT manufacturers expressed their dissatisfaction and local governments reported back that several foreign investors in the IT industry wanted to withdraw their investments, which would have been unfavorable to local development. After making international comparisons, I suggested that we had to consider not just the lost profits (or the increased costs) of foreign manufacturers as a result of reducing the tax rebate, but that we should also consider the weight of the Chinese market for international companies. We had to compare the cost efficiency of the Chinese market with that of other markets. If the problem were considered from this perspective, it would very easy to see clearly whether the views of these IT manufacturers were reasonable.

In another example, through my research on tax revenue policies in relation to foreign parties, I came to the conclusion that not only do we need to consider the benefits for different populations within our country, we must also consider the benefits and policy direction for the State, as well as the political and economic benefits and background of other countries. Only then can policies be formulated that comply with international regulations and practices, but also serve to fully protect our country's interests and seek to find a balance in the demands of our different communities. From this basis these policies can be used to promote the cooperative development of an economic society.

RETURN TO THE FURNACE: "REVIEW THE OLD TO LEARN THE NEW"[11]

I worked for 20 years after graduating from university and then returned to school as an on-the-job doctoral student. Some believe that on-the-job studies are merely "gilding" for the student and profit for the school. Admittedly, there are some students who undertake such studies not to improve their cultural awareness, to renew and augment their knowledge or strengthen their work ability. Rather, they are simply looking to add a label to their title and to make themselves appear better on paper. I believe that the results depend on the attitude with which a person approaches studies. After four years of doctoral studies at Peking University, I believe more than ever in the need for a "return to the furnace to cast the steel" through further education.

As Comrade Mao Zedong suggested:

> Those with book knowledge must develop in practical aspects; only then can they avoid stopping at the book level and avoid the errors of dogmatism. People with work experience must turn to theoretical aspects and study diligently; only then can they bring rationality and synthesis to their experience and ascend to the theoretical level; only then can they avoid the errors of empiricism.[12]

Studying should comply with the epistemology of dialectical materialism: practice, learn, practice again and learn more. This form of spiral ascendance in a never-ending revolving cycle becomes the process by which we understand the present, face the world, explore the future and constantly strive to surpass ourselves. Each cycle of practice and learning enables us to reach a higher state. "A person's knowledge is like climbing a ladder; the view becomes wider with each step."[13] Because students lack practical experience during their initial university studies, most cannot fully understand the theoretical knowledge they memorize; in their work after they graduate, they may gain an abundance of social experience and face multitudes of problems but they are often unable to generalize or make advances in their theoretical knowledge. The main purpose of "returning to the furnace to cast the steel" is to review and combine practical experience, to study new theories and to resolve the difficulties faced at work. This makes it possible to turn the notion of "learn to" —which embraces the traditional idea of becoming skilled artisans with the adaptability to deal with problems of the here and now—into "can learn"—that is, studying for originality, enhancing the ability to discover and absorb new knowledge in order to anticipate and handle changes that will arise in the future.

In my experience, genuinely learning something and improving oneself through studying while working must be done in three ways:

- Firstly, establish the idea that study is work. Studying and working are not contradictory; in fact, they are complementary activities. It requires work to strengthen our studies and it requires studies to advance in our work. A good train of thought, a good method or a good decision is often generated and perfected through studying, whereas an answer to a question, a strategic direction or relevant knowledge is often produced and captured through work. Continuous studies whilst at work can produce new awareness and new understanding in our work; associating related work with studies can bring a deeper level of understanding to the content of our studies and allow it to sink in more quickly. For this reason, one must view studying as work when engaged in on-the-job studies; one should aim at improving the quality and level of one's work, through self-evaluation and resolving major theoretical issues faced in the workplace.

- Secondly, establish the idea that studying is living. Studying is a high-standard, high-quality way of life; it is a self-regulating exercise that continuously improves our mental models; it is a physically and mentally joyful process to experience and embrace. Whilst engaged in on-the-job studies, students who are willing to learn will be provided with new opportunities. They have only to grasp and dedicate themselves to these opportunities, study industriously and excel as a student to attain the full essence and happiness that life has to offer.

- Thirdly, establish the idea that studying is a long-term mission. Some may be in a rush to be successful; they are impatient and hot-tempered, wanting to achieve everything in an instant. They are in such a hurry that they oversimplify and swallow the knowledge too quickly so that it is not properly digested. Self-improvement is not an instantaneous process; it takes concerted effort over time and through imperceptible influences; and sometimes it requires that you review the old to learn the new. Clearly, you will need to burn the midnight oil in order to pass an examination, but the ultimate test is how to improve on your overall quality and research skills, and how to generate originality.

Clearly, studying for a doctorate while working is a challenge that requires self-discipline and energy. As a middle-aged person entering this arena for learning, I experienced great pressure as well as happiness. In particular, being surrounded by the vigor of youth, I had an unprecedented sense of panic. I felt that I could not afford to be the slightest bit complacent, and instead kept my head down and forged ahead. My four years of receiving the torch from my teachers could be likened to the poet who "whilst often collecting the finest blossoms from the garden of literature . . . was able to see both near and far."[14] I could only hope to get a slight glimpse into the great depths of knowledge and wisdom in the fields of political and financial studies.

My studies at Peking University also provided me with further understanding of how to strengthen my innovation skills. Previously, I had always thought that such skills were a product of advancement in overall quality and the continual renewal and augmentation of knowledge. I had thought that it came from studying and constant learning. Gradually, I came to realize that innovation skills are also created by the requirements of work, stimulated by work duties and attitude towards work. Now, I was aware that these two criteria were insufficient and that innovation skills can also come from the results of interaction and the interaction of results. Consequently, not only did I throw even more energy into my studies and my work, but I also endeavored to closely combine the two. Not only did I actively combine my own knowledge, pay close attention to the key teachings of my professors and learn from books, but I also actively participated in mutual exchange and discussion with elite students in my class. In particular, when analyzing typical cases, teachers and students would express their own understanding of the matter based on their respective life experiences, which allowed me to see the case from all angles and many different perspectives. It seemed as if suddenly I was seeing "the real face of Lushan Mountain"[15] from a greater height.

Additionally, my studies produced two effects: Firstly, it provided motivation to my daughter who, once admitted into Peking University, pursued her studies with the enthusiasm and energy of a high school third grader, not once relenting. Secondly, it motivated my colleagues. People who worked in the units under my responsibility witnessed that I used almost all my spare time outside of an already busy work life to study, and naturally many were spurred on to engage in their own renewal and augmentation of knowledge.

TO STUDY, ONE MUST UNDERSTAND THE METHOD OF INPUT AND OUTPUT

Anton Chekhov said, "Method is talent's sister." One could say that studying without researching one's methods is studying without complete significance. China has a strong tradition of placing emphasis on being adept learners. Consider, for example, the lines:

> The skillful learner, while the master seems indifferent, makes double the attainments of another, and ascribes the merit to the master. The unskillful learner, while the master is diligent with him, makes only half the attainments of another, and is dissatisfied with the master.[16]

During my studies I was deeply aware of the rare opportunity I had been granted but I was also aware that time was limited and that, in turn, made me keenly aware of the importance of methodology in studying.

During my studies, I mainly focused on the following study methods:

- **First, balance extensive reading and specialized study.** In my experience, you must have a systematic and connected grasp of the knowledge and theories related to your profession. Secondly, you must also be able to look at things from the reverse side and take a critical look at the accepted theories with a view to breaking through the limitations of the already known. In addition, you must adopt a position based on the synthesis of multiple disciplines to investigate knowledge and the trends of the problem being researched.

  What counts as "specialization"? My understanding is that it is primarily to penetrate a subject through studying. "The methodology of studying is to learn in proper sequence in order to be proficient."[17] Secondly, you must draw on past experiences and lessons to reflect and reach conclusions at a higher level. You must do your utmost to seek extended meaning, to discover and to originate. Only if you couple specialization with erudition during the course of your studies will you achieve results that outweigh the effort.

- **Secondly, think more and refine your writing.** The great thinkers of the past tell us that "The path to learning is based on thought"[18] and that "Learning without thinking is labor lost."[19] Only by reflecting on what you learn during your studies will you come to a deeper understanding and be able to absorb it in a way that enriches the body of your experience and knowledge.

  However, the spark of thought can be transient and can be easily forgotten. For this reason, you need to make a record of the fruits of your thinking, constantly revising and refining them. Through a never-ending cycle of re-thinking and re-refinement, you can learn to extract the essence of learned knowledge and allow it to permeate the core of your being. Thinking without writing is akin to words without deeds; writing without refining is like giving up halfway through, or working on something half-heartedly. An important path to learning how to think lies in mastering correct methods of thinking. In my studies, I used to employ both divergent and convergent thinking. The former involves the use of the imagination to open up the train of thought to all directions, breaking through constraints to consider issues from multiple viewpoints to discover other, fresher, possible solutions, assumptions and methods. The latter method places an issue at the center and uses differing perspectives to analyze the ins and outs of the issue and to clear away the mist surrounding it and to unearth its true face.

  For example, when considering the issue of debt, I underwent five learning stages: The harms of money lending; the benefits of money lending; the notion of higher short-term gain to the detriment of the long-term; higher gain and lower harm and conforming to trends; and discretionary approaches. During the whole thought process I made sure to note down every idea that came to me, as well as any questions raised by others, and then I set out to seek evidence and solutions, to consider the issues on a deeper level. After many revisions, the theory that I wrote about proactive financial policies was received positively by critics and has been the basis of further research as China continues its efforts towards preparing for financial policy adjustment.

- **Thirdly, focus and determination.** "When a gentleman learns, he hears with his ears, remembers in his heart, spreads it throughout his being and demonstrates it with his actions."[20] Under the shock of the tidal wave of the market economy, some people have lost their way. Their desire to better themselves is less resolute; they wallow in self-indulgence and thoughtless gambling, becoming enthralled in a world of debauchery and corruption.

  Studying is like attempting to scale new heights on a mountain: It takes passion, technique and a great deal of willpower. I use the word "focus" here to convey the need to eliminate outside temptation, to endure loneliness and to study diligently. "Determination" is the spirit of perseverance. You can't afford to be half-hearted or impatient, rushing ahead looking for quick rewards. Undoubtedly, the pressures of work and family will dampen the natural enthusiasm and energy for studying; and the distractions of everyday life can often erode industriousness and willpower. My view is that, since you have chosen a remote destination, you must plough ahead through the wind and rain. Over the years, my method of snatching a little leisure in a busy life sustained my drive during my doctoral studies. When others were playing cards over the dinner table, I used my time to study, accumulating small achievements and enriching my life along the way.

- **Mastering the subject.** "To study well, one must understand the method of input and output; at the beginning, one must seek to take all in and at the end one must look to let all out."[21] In striving to master the subject, I took care to nurture and practise four abilities throughout the course of my studies. First was the ability to conclude and summarize, cutting out superfluous details to find the essential structure—the spine and skeleton—of the subject and expressing the connections found within complex content in a few precise words. A second, and related, ability was that of using the essential points to build a knowledge system that encapsulated the whole picture. Qi Baishi said that "In painting a bird, it takes 10 years to show its physical form and another 10 years to show its spiritual form." In my experience, studying is a bit like this in that the third ability required is that of being able to work from individual cases to find the norm; to move from the concrete to the abstract and from the superficial to the essence; to extract general rules from specific instances. In this way, the barriers of the old concepts are removed, revealing new paths.

Fourth was the ability to analyze and solve problems. The ability to really grasp knowledge and make it useful was often largely related to writing frequently. Whilst studying, I would often write two types of small thesis. The first would be an elaboration of an existing view or perspective but in my own words. The other was a more creative approach, in that it involved editing, enriching and developing on previous ideas that people had had and slightly advancing on this knowledge in order to add, in some small way, to the general understanding of the matter at hand.

TACKLING KEY ISSUES: HEAVEN REWARDS THE DILIGENT

My doctoral studies were not all plain sailing; there were torrents and rocky waters too. My biggest challenge and most painful experiences were related to mastering English and completing my final dissertation. These challenges took me to the edge of exhaustion. However, when I eventually came through on the other side, I was rewarded with lasting benefits.

The difficulties I face as a student in my forties and not having basic English skills were even greater than I had imagined. No tricks were available to me by which I could become proficient at listening, speaking, reading and writing; my only weapon was a willingness to work at it doggedly. Every day after work I studied English by myself. Even when I had to work until 9 PM, I would remain behind to do my exercises before going home. For three and a half years I did not take a single weekend off. My fellow students set up a small English study group and would devote three half days at the weekend and one evening a week to studying English under the tuition of a fellow student. We kept up our English group for two years and most of the students managed to pass their English proficiency tests. Because I needed to ask for more time off than the others, my level was still quite poor, and I was still unable to pass the tests. For this reason, I asked an English graduate student from the Beijing Broadcasting Institute to be my home tutor for a year and a half, and she tutored me four times a week. No matter how late I had to work, she would always wait for me to finish so that we could have our lesson.

I remember one Friday evening during the preparations for an APEC Finance Ministers Meeting I accompanied leaders to check on the conference preparations in Suzhou and we remained busy there until 2 AM on Sunday. We had originally planned to take the morning off to rest and return to Beijing in the afternoon, but I got up at 4 AM and traveled to Shanghai where I could catch a 6 o'clock flight back to Beijing to attend my English lesson at Peking University. When I walked into the classroom looking as if I had not slept a wink, the teacher and my classmates gave me a standing ovation. I started to have presbyopia earlier than I should have because of my English studies. One of the reasons for this was that the type in the English books was too small and I used to joke that "all our English dictionaries and reference books were made for young people, the text is so small; it would be strange if I did not have presbyopia! No wonder people say you shouldn't study after 40!"

However, during the SARS outbreak, I suspended my English studies for over a year because of all sorts of abnormal pressures and increased workload. Not surprisingly, I lost a lot of what I had learned and I was extremely disappointed and hurt that I had not been able to keep it up. I made a resolution to give it one more go. I want to use this opportunity today to emphasize to you all that the critical part of studying English is to stay committed and to persevere over years if necessary.

Another huge trial for me was the writing of the final doctoral dissertation, the grand finale of a doctoral degree, and Peking University is well known for its demanding requirements in this regard. Writing a dissertation is akin to bearing a child, in that the process of labor is particularly painful. My dissertation underwent through three major revisions. Initially, I had chosen to write on the subject of government debt, starting from the Glorious Revolution in England all the way up to the hot topic of the day, which was the problem of the Chinese government's huge arrears in export tax rebate payments.

After I submitted my proposal, caring professors pointed out to me that my chosen subject area was too politically sensitive and, in consideration of my standing, suggested that I carry out research in my field of work, rather than researching a theoretical topic. Abandoning my first choice, I then picked the "history and future of public finances" as my topic. In this, I planned to investigate the creation and evolution of the public finance system and to analyze its future direction. I was quite interested in history and liked researching historical issues, so I already had a foundation for my topic. I found it easy to write about the past but writing on present and future strategic development was more difficult. However, my professors thought that the comparisons of western and eastern public finance developments were too large for the dissertation and suggested that I should focus on the future trends of public finances. On this basis I set my dissertation topic as "The construction and expansion of the public finance sector of China in her transformation period." During the anonymous evaluation of my dissertation, I was advised that I should strengthen and combine political and financial theories and use the theories on institutional change relevant in political science as a precursor and foundation to analyze issues of public finance. Subsequently, I made another large revision to my dissertation, striving to pinpoint the pulse of China's economic and social development through integrating the overall trends within the rapidly changing economy and society and analyzing the major issues involved in the construction and future directions of a public finance sector. The dissertation described and discussed the key elements related to public finance in theoretical research, institutional research, mechanism research, policy research and research within an international context, and it finally passed the open defense stage.

As the Tang dynasty poet Du Fu (712–770) said, "A piece of writing lasts a thousand years, the gain and loss are known to the author's heart." I have many emotions and mixed feelings whilst reflecting on the experience of writing and revising my dissertation. I had always thought of myself as someone who enjoyed research and contemplation; my work has always been closely related to writing and most of the reports that I have written have been used as the framework and basic content of various policies. Though I would never dare underestimate what was involved, I did not think that writing a dissertation would present me with great difficulty. I did not realize that the process would be so complicated or that it would be so closely scrutinized. In the final notes of the dissertation, I expressed my gratitude to the professors who had given me so much assistance:

> Their ideas and suggestions were as precious as gold. Their criticism and comments were things that I rarely encounter as an "official." Not only were they extremely significant in the direction of the revisions and improvements made to my dissertation, but they have also provided a significant direction to my future work and studies.

It is certainly true that the great challenges presented by the process of researching and writing this work have enabled me to analyze problems more deeply, and have strengthened my ability to research financial strategy in relation to the political theory that I have learned. Now I understand that the emphasis placed on research by those at Peking University is not just the topic of a lesson, but is also excellent training in willpower and self-cultivation. I realize that the acquisition of knowledge is no easy task, but at the same time I realize the joy of being a scholar.

THERE IS NO END TO LEARNING AND WE SHOULD CHERISH TIME

In the time between the defense of my dissertation and the graduation ceremony, I took part in three events in quick succession. The first was a visit to the Ministry of Finance's De Cai Kindergarten on Children's Day to watch the children perform for the special holiday;[22] the second was to take part in a memorial service; and the third was to participate in a special meeting on the issue of preserving Chairman Mao's personal belongings in a Memorial Museum in Shaoshan. These events prompted to a greater appreciation of the words: "Time is a fleeting guest; a hundred years will pass in the blink of an eye."[23] Life is so beautiful and yet so brief; what were we before we were born and what will we become after our death?

Life and death are unavoidable rules of nature and thus we should accept them calmly and face up to them; after all, a calm and peaceful mind is better than a sick and worried one. Given how fleeting and precious life is, I believe we must devote our limited time to work for society, to do our utmost to spread more material and spiritual wealth amongst others. We must allow the value of our own creativity to enrich each part of our lives and those of our family and friends, and make a greater contribution to the work of the mother-land we love.

I remember reading a book titled *Tuesdays with Morrie*, which tells of an American sociologist, Professor Morrie Schwartz, who remained magnanimous and calm throughout his suffering from an incurable disease that was racking his body. In the last days of his life, this kind-hearted and wise old man would meet every Tuesday with a former pupil of his to discuss life issues. These meetings lasted for 14 weeks. He told his student, "For life to have real meaning, you must commit yourself to love, commit yourself to those around you . . . and give things to others that you ought to give."[24] I thought at the time: think how wonderful it would be if we started life old and became younger! At least we would not take as many wrong turns. Of course, this is impossible. So, how do we make up for this? After the three visits I spoke of earlier, I started to find an answer to this question. It is to consult more with others, reach more conclusions from lessons learned and contemplate problems more deeply! All of these depend upon studying diligently, reading more and thinking deeply.

There is an ancient saying: "Wisdom takes learning and learning therefore is knowledge."[25] Studying is a basic tool for human existence and social development. It is also an endless, lifelong pursuit that accompanies one through life. I have explained it before this way: Knowledge is less than learning, learning is less than thinking, thinking is less than creativity, one-time creativity is less than having core competitiveness, and lifelong learning is the source and driving force of a core competitiveness. Although different people will have differing interpretations of the meaning of lifelong learning, I believe that its root and nature can be grasped by the following essential points:

First, just as Xun Zi wrote in *On Learning*: "There is no end to learning." Any person who wishes to avoid aging in mind, becoming rigid in thought or losing their abilities must view study as an unending process and must not see it as something that can be achieved once and for all. You have to learn amid changes and growth throughout your life, in order to meet the challenges presented by new knowledge and new environments.

Confucius said that men of noble character must not restrict themselves to one special field of knowledge or skill but, instead, should learn many disciplines to a higher level and develop their whole being. Lifelong learning is not a simple concept of education or learning, but a type of social behavior and a particular way of life. It requires that society build comprehensive systems and mechanisms for lifelong learning to resolve the questions that people ask regarding what and how to study.

Third, that the emphasis should be on the student's self-motivation and autonomy. "One can only make an effort once one is aware of learning, and one can be expected to make progress in studies once one makes an effort."[26] The quality and results of a person's studies are determined by the attitude, methods and abilities he brings to bear. Having a real grasp of the benefits of lifelong learning is the only way to counter the ups and downs and the frustrations that are an integral part of the study process. For me, studying is an enjoyable pastime; so much so that I do not hesitate to use it as a reason to be excused from dinner engagements. Often, I am met with a response such as: "I just don't see the point of why you are still studying!" But if they don't get it, they don't get it. I find racking my brains over a particular problem much more interesting than having to find something to say, just for the sake of it, around the banquet table. Some of my friends who see me working day and night on my writing and not taking the holidays to rest caringly suggest that I find a better balance between work and leisure, and find more time to relax. They do not realize that, for me, writing—particularly the writing I do outside of work—is a way of letting off steam and a release; it is a way to relax and recharge myself.

There is an ancient Chinese proverb: "Learning is like rowing upstream; not to advance is to drop back." The philosophy contained in this proverb underscores the concept of lifelong learning today. It applies to whole units as well as to individuals. Based on my own ideas and learning results, I proposed a training program for my work unit comprising "self-reflection, learning from others and preparation for the future" aimed at the three levels of official postings within sections, divisions and departments. After it was accepted and put into place, the civil servants in our unit changed their approach towards training. Where training was once merely a duty, now they fall over each other to sign up and those preparing for promotion examinations wouldn't miss even half a day's training.

I believe that lifelong learning and scientific study are an important element of a nation's development. This view was reinforced at the Sixteenth Party Congress, where the strategic task of "forming a learning society where all citizens learn and lifelong learning is promoted" was put forward. The third plenary meeting of the Congress proposed the objectives to "build a modern education system for the people and systems for lifelong learning and to create a learning society." In this spirit, the central leadership of the new government took the initiative and set an example. Between December 2002 and November 2004, the Political Bureau of the Central Committee organized a total of 16 collective study programs to promote the notion of a learning society, and gained wide-reaching public attention and praise. With the support of the Central Committee, the enthusiasm for studying was raised and sustained across the nation. We are right now in the midst of re-making an ancient country, with thousands of years of flourishing literature and generations of talent, into a new nation of learning. The profound scholarly nature of the Chinese people will allow us to move forward on a majestic path.

THE FUTURE: A MAN OF NOBLE CHARACTER FINDS STRENGTH WITHIN IN THE COURSE OF VICISSITUDES

Just as a person's attitude can determine his life, so too can a nation's spirit determine its prosperity or decline. An individual's struggles and a nation's prosperous development both require a positive, enthusiastic spirit, a tenacious and unyielding fighting spirit and an indefatigable spirit for learning. Mao Zedong's heroic words of "confidently believing that man can live for two hundred years, and so can swim an accumulated length of three thousand miles" are truly a vivid portrayal of an indomitable resilience and untiring energy.

I believe that to be resilient and untiring, one must embrace the following four qualities:

First, we must struggle for advancement, working robustly and conscientiously. When discussing the way of political studies, *The Doctrine of Mean*[27] points out:

> If someone can do one thing after learning one time, and I cannot do the same, then I will learn it a hundred times; if someone can do one thing after learning ten times, and I cannot do the same, then

I will learn it a thousand times. If you can really follow this, idle can become bright and soft can become strong no matter how frail you are.

This sheds light on the struggle for advancement, the strength to recover from setbacks and an energetic and promising spirit. Thinking about this, I realized that, although there were many doctoral students and many government officials among my former classmates in university, there are actually very few officials who have gone on to further academic achievement. In the 20 years after graduation, what were they doing with their spare time outside of work? When they attained some success or faced difficulties, did they find a way to keep moving forward or did they simply give up?

Second, in order to keep up with the times, we must eliminate the old and establish the new. The world's development is progressing more rapidly with each passing day. If we stay bound by old conventions, allow ourselves to be stuck inside old wisdom, paint a fixed picture, do not reassess our surroundings, or if we just focus on our own professional success, treat doctoral studies as "gilding" and are not willing to exert real effort, study hard or instigate reform, then we will always fall behind others.

Looking back and comparing the essays I wrote before and after my doctoral studies, I can detect two major differences: My reasoning skills have got better and my ability to initiate ideas has been strengthened. Some of my friends have commented on the improvement, which I believe is because my essays are now more comprehensive, more direct and based more on my own reasoning to identify problems for myself, rather than simply expounding on other people's words and ideas.

There is another matter that I believe can well demonstrate the importance of innovation and that is the creation of accounting and auditing software assessment systems. In 1990, when I was Division Director for Division I of the Accounting Department, the marketplace for accounting and auditing software was a real mess, with so many bad products available along with the good. With the support of our leaders and with the assistance of our colleagues, we took on the much-needed task of preparing an evaluation of the quality and legality of accounting and auditing software to assist users in making their choice. We established an evaluation and administrative system for the commercialization of accounting and auditing software. The structure we put in place for the commercialization of the Chinese market for audit software remains in force to this day.

Third, we must remain independent in character and pursue justice. In his *Sorrow of Separation*, Qu Yuan wrote: "But since my heart did love such purity, I'd regret not a thousand deaths to die." This steadfastness of character in pursuing justice and truth of which he spoke is still held in high regard today. When the new China was created it was poor and underdeveloped; to change this, people had to rely on their own strength and not depend on the support of others. Deng Xiaoping said, "China's issues must be dealt with according to the Chinese people's circumstances; they depend on the people's own strength. Being self-reliant always has been, is and will be in the future a foothold of the Chinese nation's pride, independence and pursuit of self-improvement."[28]

Only by establishing a strong autonomous consciousness will China be better able to protect its independence, dignity and interests. I believe that in order to be independent and to pursue justice, we must continuously study. Only with more knowledge will we be better equipped to make comparisons and judgments, come closer to knowing right from wrong and justice from injustice. Only people with great experience know that many situations cannot be judged simply by relying on emotion or past experience, and that relying on one theory, area of knowledge or skill also has great limitations. Only by synthesizing knowledge from multiple disciplines can we produce a more reliable identification of a problem.

Fourth, we need to display fortitude and to see things more philosophically. During his travels, Confucius encountered many obstacles but even when his own life was in danger, he stuck to his principles, demonstrating the unyielding spirit of doing the impossible. The poets tell us that "A person who experienced a hard life can achieve anything."[29] My personal experience confirms this view. I was brought up by my paternal grandparents in the countryside during the time of the "Down to the Countryside" movement. The hardships experienced then taught me to accept and face up to the challenges and changes we encountered in life. They also made me learn to embrace and be passionate about my destiny, to enrich myself by rising above the commonplace. I often compare myself to my high school classmates. In my school, there were four classes at my level, with approximately 200 students. At the time, only I managed to be admitted into university. In the high school examinations of 1978, our county had about 2,500 students taking liberal arts examinations. I was ranked third with my results, but of the four enrolled undergraduate students only I scored well enough to get into a university outside the province. Now, I am the only one who is in Beijing working for the central government. What is the reason for this? I know that I am no more intelligent than others, but apart from luck and the assistance of others, maybe it is because I am more fond of studying and have such a love for learning that I was a bit more determined.

In July 2004 at the Peking University doctoral graduation ceremony, a Doctor of Laws gave an emotional speech that moved me deeply. She said that she had been pursuing her studies at the University for a decade, from being an undergraduate all the way through to her doctoral degree, and now was reluctant to have to make her departure from her alma mater. In the silence of the night, she said, she had walked slowly around the Nameless Lake, kneeled devoutly at the lakeside and kissed the earth that had given her sustenance for the past 10 years.

By the time my own diploma was handed out, I couldn't stop myself from giving the degree certificate a big kiss. The four years of my doctoral studies were momentary in the length of a lifetime. I often think that a person can live in the same place for so many years, and though familiar with every blade of grass and every tree, not be moved by it. There are other places, however, that create love at first sight, in which one can rapidly become absorbed, creating a strong sense of belonging, recognition and bonding, and to which one will stay faithful until the end.

"Today I am proud because of Peking University, tomorrow Peking University will be proud of me". This is the slogan hung on all sides of the University campus; it expresses its aspirations for its future graduates and is a repeated encouragement for the students. I know that it is next to impossible to make Peking University proud of me, but all the same I am working hard to please the University and, at the very least, not to disappoint her. For this reason, the end of my student life at Peking University became the beginning of my new journey.

The Xiamen National Accounting Institute is also fertile soil for learning. You too will be able to paint fresher, more beautiful pictures. I wholeheartedly hope that you will all seize the opportunity to study diligently and turn your three years of study into a wider, more even path to your future and to provide a more stable and resilient foundation.

ENDNOTES

1 Edited version of the speech given at the Inaugural Ceremony of the First Program of Master of Professional Accounting (MPAcc), at Xiamen National Accounting Institute, March 25, 2005.

2 The phrase "on-the-job graduate students" is used to indicate graduate students who are studying for a postgraduate degree while in full-time employment.

3 Refers to the period in the late 1960s and early 1970s when educated urban youth went to work in the countryside or mountain areas in response to Chairman Mao Zedong's call to be re-educated by peasants.

4 *Groaning Words* by Ming Lü Kun.

5 Zhang Zhongxing 1986, *Fu Xuan Suo Hua (Chatting while Basking in the Sun)*, Harbin: Heilongjiang People's Press: 84.

6 Chen Pingyuan 1998, *Story of Old Peking University*, Nanjing: Jiangsu Cultural Press: 29.

7 Henry Rosovsky 1996, *American Campus Culture* (translated version by Xie Zong Xian *et al.*) Jinan: Shandong People's Press: 82.

8 Shorthand for the call that the Communist Party of China (CPC) provides insight and leadership for economic and cultural progress, and commits itself to public good. Former CPC General Secretary Jiang Zemin, who was credited with its creation, literally admonished his comrades to "represent the development trend of China's most advanced productive forces, the orientation of China's most advanced culture, and the fundamental interests of the overwhelming majority of the Chinese people." The theory is the result of deliberations of the CPC's third-generation leaders on legitimacy and Party-building. At the Sixteenth CPC National Congress in 2002, it was formally written into the Party Constitution.

9 The Scientific Development Concept is the current official guiding socioeconomic ideology of the Communist Party of China incorporating sustainable development, social welfare, a person-centered society, increased democracy, and, ultimately, the creation of a harmonious society. It is lauded by the Chinese government as a successor and ideological extension to Marxism-Leninism, Mao Zedong Thought, Deng Xiaoping Theory and the "Three Represents." Credit for the theory is given to current Chinese leader Hu Jintao and his administration, who took power in 2002. It is the newest brand added to the idea of socialism with Chinese characteristics ratified into the Communist Party of China's constitution at the Seventeenth Party Congress in October 2007.

10 These include: "Resolutely implementing 'The Three Represents' and making great strides towards prosperity—sights and thoughts on a trip to the Philippines;" "Each generation produces its own talents—a thorough

analysis of how the world's powerful nations have flourished and their implications for China's development;" "White and Black—reflections from a visit to South Africa;" "Life and Death—reflections from a visit to Egypt;" and "Walls and Bridges—reflections from a visit to Hungary."

11 From the *Analects of Confucius* (551–497 BC).

12 *Selected readings from the works of Mao Zedong*, Beijing: People's Press, 1986.

13 *Collected Works of and Quotes from Lu Xiangshan.*

14 Li E (1692–1752), *Notes on Song Poetry.*

15 This is adapted from a line in a poem by Li Bai (701–762)—"He fails to see what Lushan Mountain really looks like because he is on the Mountain himself"— and means the truth about someone or something.

16 *The Classic of Rites, Record on the Subject of Education.*

17 From *Yang Zheng Yi Gui* (Rules handed down for properly educating children).

18 Chao Yuezhi, *Chao Shi Ke Yu (Analects of previous people by Chao of Song Dynasty).*

19 *The Analects of Confucius, On Governing.*

20 Xun Zi, *On Learning.*

21 Chen Shan, *Men Shi Yu.*

22 June 1.

23 Xu Hun: *Nan Xiang Ye Zuo, Yi Kai Yuan Chan Ding Er Dao Zhe (Sitting in a Pavilion in the Evening and Thinking about Buddhism).*

24 Mitch Albom, *Tuesdays with Morrie*, translated by Wu Hong, Shanghai: Shanghai Foreign Press, 1998.

25 Wang Chong, *Lun Heng (Discourses Weighed in the Balance).*

26 Zhang Zai, *Zheng Meng* (Educating Children), Chapter 8: *Zhong Zheng Pian* (Chapter of Honesty).

27 This is one of the Four Books, part of the Confucian canonical scriptures. The composition of the text is attributed to the only grandson of Confucius. The purpose of the book is to demonstrate the usefulness of a golden way to gain perfect virtue. It focuses on the "way" (Tao) that is prescribed by a heavenly mandate to everyone. Following these heavenly instructions by learning and teaching will automatically result in a Confucian virtue.

28 Deng Xiaoping, *Deng Xiaoping's collected essays (1975–82)*, Beijing People's Press, 1983: 72.

29 Lü Benzhong, *Shi You (*Miscellanea about teachers and friends).

Chapter 2

"Uphold Morality on Strong Shoulders and Create Brilliant Writings with a Fine Hand"[1]

Despite the freezing weather of this dreary season, I feel a sense of warmth that fills me with thoughts of spring. Your passion, your thirst for knowledge and your determination to achieve progress has inspired me. In you lie our hopes for an outstanding performance for the senior accounting talent training program and the flourishing of the national accountancy profession!

Before I begin, I would like to convey to you two messages from the Party Leadership Group of the Ministry of Finance. **The first is one of warm congratulations** on the successful commencement of classes for the present phase of the program, and to each of you for having been selected from the very many candidates wishing to take part in the program. I am deeply aware that it was not easy for you to get this "admission ticket," which is the culmination of many years of hard work, diligent research and the sweat and blood poured out into your studies. **The second is heartfelt thanks.** We would like to thank the Shanghai National Accounting Institute and the relevant units within the Ministry for their huge contributions towards the Phase 1 Training Program, and we would like to thank all of you, as well as our multitude of comrades who are fighting a fierce battle on the accounting battlefield, for your warm support and participation in the program. We would like to further thank all of you for your long-term loyalty and dedication to the accountancy profession in our country.

You are the elite—the pillars—of the accounting world. In the course of this speech I hope that I can encourage and motivate each of you to continue to study and understand the thoughts of the CPC Central Committee and the State Council regarding the strategy to strengthen the country through implementing the accounting talent program. I hope that all of you can persevere in your learning, continually improve your abilities, and vigorously promote the spirit of China's accounting with honesty and trustworthiness, objectivity and impartiality, open-mindedness and innovation. Armed with deep theoretical qualities, broad international perspectives, outstanding professional standards and excellent working abilities, you can contribute your dedication, wisdom and toil towards promoting the development of the accounting profession and the construction of a prosperous and harmonious socialist society.

TO ENSURE THE SUCCESS OF THE ACCOUNTANCY PROFESSION, WORK FOR THE URGENT IMPLEMENTATION OF THE ACCOUNTING TALENT STRATEGY

Proverbs such as "the key to governing lies in getting good people" and "those who gain good people will be strong, while those who lose good people will perish", which have been passed down from generation to generation, speak of the same truth: The extent to which a country, an industry or a unit can continually train and attract outstanding talent will to a large extent determine the success or failure of that country, industry or unit.

As you are all aware, the first unified feudal dynasty in the history of China was the Qin dynasty which, after more than 30 monarchs and a few hundred years of vicissitudes as a small vassal state on the western border during the later years of the Zhou dynasty, was able to gain control over all its enemies and annex their lands. The key factor in this transformation was the ability to attract and use good talent. Duke Mu, for example, obtained the services of You Yu from the west and of Bai

Lixi from the city of Wan in the east. He welcomed Jian Shu from the state of Sung and requested the services of Gong Sun Zhi from the state of Jin. As a result of having these capable generals and ministers, he was able to carry out many exploits to benefit the country, expand his territory by thousands of miles, and defeat the barbarians in the western regions. During the time of Duke Xiao, there was Shang Yang, an important statesman of Qin in the Warring States Period, who introduced political reforms to strengthen the country. Ying Zheng, who was king of the Qin from 246 BCE to 221 BCE during the Warring States Period, had military generals such as Wang Ben and Meng Tian and civil ministers such as Lü Buwei and Li Si at his disposal. Because he had so many talented individuals from all generations from the State of Qin, he was able to unify the nation and achieve prosperity.

Of course, this is only one of a multitude of examples, and the fact that talented individuals are the basis for achieving success applies both to China and foreign nations and to ancient times as well as contemporary times. Since we entered the twenty-first century, the world has been developing in a multi-faceted manner; economic globalization has been increasing, scientific progress is advancing tremendously, and talented individuals have become the most valuable strategic resource and are playing an increasingly important role in determining overall national competitiveness. The emergence of a batch of outstanding talent can often lead a unit forward, revitalize an industry, and open up a completely new sector. Their importance is self-evident. Human talent constitutes the foundation for prosperity and success; and the rise and fall of talented people can affect the fortunes of the country.

The spring wind brings the blossoming of the peaches and plums, and nourishes the lands. The new Central Collective Leadership of the CPC, of which our comrade Hu Jintao is the general secretary, attaches great importance to the talent development in meeting the various challenges and new circumstances of the new century. In December 2003, Hu Jintao pointed out at the CPC Central Committee Talent Project Forum that we need to approach the matter from a high-level strategic perspective, and recognize the urgency of the strategy to strengthen the country. After the forum, the CPC Central Committee and the State Council issued the "Decision regarding further strengthening the talent development." They proposed that:

> [I]n the major task of constructing China's unique socialism, talent
> must be regarded as the key factor for promoting the progress of the

aforesaid task, and we must diligently nurture many high-quality workers and many professional talents . . . who are proficient at carrying out innovation . . . [and] open up a new scenario where batches . . . of talent are produced and . . . used to their utmost, to transform our country and improve our country's core competitiveness and integrated national strength.

Recently, the "Suggestions of the CPC Central Committee regarding the formulation of the Eleventh Five-Year Plan for the national economic and societal development" passed at the fifth plenary meeting of the Sixteenth CPC Central Committee further emphasized the need to "strengthen the construction of human resource capabilities" and to implement the project for the training of talent in three specific areas: Political talent for the party, administrative and managerial talent for the enterprises, and professional technical talent.

These statements and conclusions were developed from a high-level perspective to establish the overall picture as we look towards the future. They provide very strong theoretical guidance and focus on current and future realities.

The Ministry of Finance has always placed great emphasis on the talent development program, particularly in the accounting training program. It is in the initial stages of setting up the systems for continual education for accountants—tests for professional technical qualifications, practicing qualifications, incentives for commendations, and ethics for the accounting profession—and this has resulted in a national education and training network that operates at different levels. This encompasses the entire country and is leading to a continual improvement in the academic and professional qualifications of the accounting professionals. This, in turn, will serve to protect and contribute towards the development of the socialist market economy in our country.

However, we must also clearly see that the current overall level of the accounting professionals in our country is not high. There is a shortage of senior accounting talent and the progress in training prospective talent is slow. The cultivation of professional ethics, professional standards, knowledge structures and overall qualities still lags the requirements for developing the socialist market economy and the demands of international competition. This has resulted in serious constraints for the reform and development of the accounting profession, and we need to solve the problem through continually deepening the reforms and introducing innovative mechanisms.

For this purpose, the party group of the Ministry of Finance has decided to implement the leading accounting talent strategy and train and select a large batch of accounting talent appropriate for current development requirements. In particular, the senior accounting talent training program is an important measure for developing the talent necessary to strengthen accounting functions, disseminating accounting policies, organizing continuing education, carrying out research into practical problems, and making use of a few experienced individuals to lead progress towards a comprehensive improvement in the overall quality of the nation's accounting team.

Just think about it: If we can mobilize the learning passion of the multitude of accountants in the country, learn from each other, help each other and surpass each other, this would energize the entire profession. The successful implementation of the accounting talent strategy is crucially connected to the strength and weakness, success and failure, and life and death of the accountancy profession. It is both a present concern that has top priority and a long-term strategy; its significance is very important and far reaching.

THE ACCOUNTING TALENT STRATEGY: AN ESSENTIAL PATHWAY TOWARD ECONOMIC AND SOCIETAL DEVELOPMENT

Since the reforms and liberalization, particularly during the 10th Five-Year Plan period, the accountancy profession in our country has stimulated development through reforms, striven for improvement through competition and achieved very significant results. The system of laws and regulations for accounting has been gradually perfected, and the accounting model based on a market economy and on a system of accounting standards has been initiated. The social status of the accountancy profession has been significantly elevated, and the accountancy profession has played an important role in strengthening economic management, improving economic efficiency, protecting the interests of the State and the general public, and promoting economic development, reforms and liberalization. The accounting team has grown in size and strength, and has produced a huge batch of outstanding representatives who are determined on carrying out reform and innovation. Recently, the Ministry of Finance has commended a batch of outstanding and excellent accountants, and the various regions and relevant departments have also launched the "double first" commendation program. This gives full recognition to the results and contributions of accountants at large in the work of reform, liberalization and modernization.

Currently, our country is entering a new phase of building an affluent society, and accelerating the promotion of economic and social development. At the fifth plenary meeting of the Sixteenth CPC Central Committee, the party determined the guiding principles, overall objectives and basic responsibilities for the economic and societal development in our country for the next five years. It also set out the requirements for the scientific development perspective to provide the leadership required to ensure that economic growth is maintained and accelerated, that capabilities for independent innovation are enhanced, that the coordinated urban and rural development is promoted, that construction of a harmonious society is accelerated, and that reform and liberalization is continually deepened.

In the strategy for that period, the CPC Central Committee has set down important guiding opinions for the further development of the accountancy profession, as well as setting higher standards. The accountancy profession must build upon the foundation of its current achievements, and continually carry out innovation of the systems, policies, mechanisms and theories that underpin it. It must deepen reforms and accelerate development, so as to adapt to the new trends, requirements and challenges of economic and social development.

For example, our country's economy is moving to an accelerated transition, and requires accounting information to play a more significant role in the allocation of resources. The development of the Chinese market into an international market requires the accountancy profession to establish itself in the domestic market and look towards the international market, bringing in foreign resources to our country and competing in foreign capital markets to provide excellent and efficient services. This will require that the process of aligning our accounting standards with international standards be accelerated.

The diversification of the funding channels for enterprises in our country and the diversification of production and management models require the accounting function to be changed from the computation of profits to the adjustment of profits. Under such circumstances, accountants in our country need a comprehensive understanding of modern economics and accounting, and this will require a qualitative leap in perspectives, knowledge and abilities, in order to keep pace with the demands and challenges of economic and social growth. Otherwise, for those who remain at the level of a bookkeeper, who are only able to excel in financial calculations, when they are faced with the major trends of information technology and marketization—even if they are financial wizards—it would be like asking them to fight a modern war with a long spear. This could only ever end in a crushing defeat. Therefore, we must draw up a long-term plan, set up effective mechanisms, and adopt a series of comprehensive actions to establish good and solid practices that will direct the accounting field toward continually improving its capabilities and standards.

IMPLEMENTING THE ACCOUNTING TALENT STRATEGY IS AN IMPORTANT FOUNDATION FOR IMPROVING ENTERPRISE MANAGEMENT AND ADMINISTRATION AND FOR IMPROVING CORE COMPETITIVENESS

Enterprises are the cornerstone of the market economy; their profitability and innovative capabilities are key indicators of a country's overall strength and competitiveness. Since the reforms and liberalization, there has been significant progress for corporate reforms in our country. Many State-owned large enterprises have undertaken the structural reforms and reorganization necessary for setting up modern enterprise systems. Further transformation of the internal management and control mechanism has strengthened the leadership and function of the State-owned sector in the national economy. However, we also need to clearly recognize that there is still a huge gap between the core competitiveness and production scale of enterprises in our country and those in developed market economies. Among the top 500 enterprises in the world in 2003, there were 192 enterprises from the United States, 150 from the European Union, 89 from Japan, and only 10 from our country (excluding Hong Kong and Taiwan). While in 2004 our representation in this group had increased to 15 enterprises, some commentators have described us as "a giant with feet of clay." This may be a little extreme, but the positioning of our enterprises is truly inconsistent with our country's status and contributions to the global economy, and indicates that there are still serious constraints to their development.

What then are the constraints for the development of our domestic enterprises? There are many possible answers to this question, but I am of the opinion that the lack of senior financial and accounting management talent constitutes one of the most important reasons. As everyone knows, for an enterprise to realize sustainable operations and achieve quantitative and qualitative expansion, the key lies in improving its core competitiveness. The fundamental factor in achieving this is the availability of high-quality talent, particularly senior accounting talent with a firm grasp of modern enterprise management and development strategies. Such people are indispensable and their absence will affect the sustainable operations and development capabilities of any enterprise.

Undoubtedly, there is a serious shortage of senior accounting talent in our country at present. Statistics show that of the approximately 520,000 accountants in the big coastal provinces, only 679—that is, 0.13 percent—possess senior accountancy qualifications. The proportion is even lower in the western regions. Even those who possess senior qualifications do not always have the necessary technical competence required to develop their enterprises. For many enterprises, it is "easy to find a thousand soldiers, but hard to find a general." While it may be possible for those operating on a small scale or running a family business to get by, those dealing with complex operations and developing towards becoming large-scale enterprises often face bottlenecks at the management level, or even reach a point where nothing is done. This is a common problem. The vigorous implementation of the accounting talent training strategy is an effective path towards the improvement of enterprise management and the removal of bottlenecks in the enterprises.

IMPLEMENTING THE ACCOUNTING TALENT STRATEGY IS AN OBJECTIVE REQUIREMENT FOR ADAPTING TO THE GLOBALIZATION OF THE ECONOMY AND THE INTERNATIONALIZATION OF ACCOUNTING

In recent years, the trend towards economic globalization has been accelerating by the day, and the breadth and depth of our country's participation in the global economy have also been continually increasing. In 2005, our country's trade dependence had reached

70 percent, which is a clear indication that we are closely connected to the global economy. This mutual dependence highlights the importance of the internationalization of both accounting standards and accounting talent.

Following the series of reforms since the "two standards and two systems,"[2] there has been significant progress in the construction of accounting standards in our country. However, the rapid development of the national economy and the continual deepening of globalization have meant that the existing accounting standards need to be further reformed and adjusted to align them with international practice. After more than a year of hard work, there has been significant progress in this area. In November this year, following several rounds of discussion and verification, the China Accounting Standards Committee and the International Accounting Standards Board issued a "joint statement on the alignment process," which indicates that the country's efforts to bring our accounting standards in line with the international standards have received international recognition.

In my view, regardless of whether we are talking about the international arena or the domestic field, accounting standards constitute the manifestation of the will of the various interested parties. From the domestic perspective, formulating the accounting standards is not only the responsibility of the Ministry of Finance. It also requires the widespread participation of various parties in society, particularly of people who have extensive practical experience in enterprise accounting work and who have high levels of theoretical understanding. At the same time, the comprehensive application of new rules and standards in the enterprises also requires high-quality personnel to organize, disseminate, promote and implement them. Without this we will have little to show for our efforts and the difficult implementation of the systems will be slowed further.

Economic globalization has meant that the competition for talent is intensifying by the day. Various countries, particularly developed countries, are implementing strategies and policies for the development and renewal of human resources. Countries like the United States, Japan and Korea have strengthened their talent strategies through enacting laws, while countries like Germany, England and Australia have been relaxing their visa and permanent-residency requirements to attract foreign talent in the high-technology field. The competition for talent is also affecting the accountancy profession. Since our country's accession to the World Trade Organization, the degree of opening up of the market for accounting services has been increasing continually, and while it has promoted the development of the accountancy profession in our country, it has also brought new challenges. For example, established large-scale international accounting firms have an obvious advantage in the competition for high-level talent. In comparison, the survival prospects of local accounting firms in our country—with their small-scale, single-facet operations and outdated knowledge structures—are grim. Faced with this intense competition for talent, we must adapt to the changes in the domestic and overseas environment, to the development requirements of economic globalization and the internationalization of accounting. We must put strong emphasis on implementing the strategy to continually improve the overall quality of the accounting professionals in our country, and thus strengthening our international competitiveness in this field.

FULLY DEVELOP CHAMPIONS OF ACCOUNTANCY, WITH THE BUILDING OF ABILITIES AS THE CORE, AND THE BUILDING OF NEW SYSTEMS AS THE BASIS

Implementation of the accounting talent strategy to strengthen the country will entail careful planning, setting up appropriate systems and innovative mechanisms, and the selection and training of various types of accounting talent. The goals must be defined and executed in a timely manner, based on the requirements of economic and societal development and the current state of the accounting professionals. For this, it is necessary to continue to perfect the systems for accounting examinations, appraisals, continuing education and professional ethics. This will involve government departments, educational institutes, employees and individuals to actively participate in the training, and implement the integration of academic education, on-the-job education and self-education. This in turn will require the integration of individual responsibility, the participation of the unit and sponsorship by the government, and the integration of the incentive, restrainting and market mechanisms, thereby promoting the healthy growth of accounting talent.

Implementation of the overall requirements of the strategy will require that the various levels of the department of finance should highlight the key points, distribute the work, and handle the selection and training of key talent. Otherwise, if we aimlessly shoot in all directions, we will end up not being able to establish a firm foothold, and may end up with nothing. In my view, the strategy can be concretely implemented at the following three levels: (i) the Ministry of Finance, the Chinese Institute of Certified Public Accountants (CICPA) and the Accounting Society of China, which are tier-one units of the CPC central government, should handle the selection and training of top-level talent, including leading accounting talents; (ii) provincial-level finance departments, societies and academic institutions should handle the selection and training of senior accounting management; and (iii) the basic-level finance departments and academic institutions should handle the selection and training of basic-level talent in the accountancy profession. In this way, everyone has clearly defined goals, clear positioning and consolidated plans, and there is a division of work under the same umbrella. This will establish clear lines of responsibility, prevent confusion and consolidate efforts to realize the strategy.

After clearly defining the division of work, the task of selecting and training leading accounting talents is the responsibility of the CPC accounting management department. If we are to perform this work well, we need to first resolve two major issues:

- Firstly, we have to decide what types of leaders the accountancy profession needs. Research into the current situation has shown that we need at least four types of leader. First, we need the senior-management category of accounting leading accounting talents for key State-owned enterprises. This category has an important function in promoting the expansion and strengthening of the enterprises and improving their core competitiveness. Second, we need accounting leading accounting talents from the CPA profession. Third, we need leaders from the educational and theoretical field in accounting (academic leaders). Fourth, we need senior accounting personnel from other key units, including administrative units, business units and other enterprises of a certain scale. At the same time, we require the various regions and departments to define the direction and emphasis for the training of accounting talent in accordance with their respective needs and circumstances. I believe that through the leadership, inspiration and influence of the various categories of leaders, we will improve the quality of the

accounting personnel and the level of accounting work throughout the entire accountancy profession.

- The second issue that needs to be resolved is how we go about
  developing leading talents. How we create effective training
  models for the profession is the key to determining the success
  or failure of the leadership training program. I believe this is
  also the issue that all of you sitting here are most concerned
  with. In this regard, the Department of Accounting, the Chinese
  Institute of Certified Public Accountants (CICPA), the Accounting Society of China and the National Accounting Institute
  have proposed a series of solutions and measures. I hope to
  combine the opinions of the various parties with some of my
  own thoughts, and discuss in greater depth some views on
  how to develop the senior-management category of leading
  accounting talents for enterprises.

Over the past year, we adopted "summarizing our own experience,
learning from other people, thinking about the future" as the theme.
The seven cycles of training sessions for the sections, departments and
offices of the Ministry of Finance were well received, with people
rushing to register. The candidates who were preparing to participate
in the examination to qualify for the training did not take even half-day
leave during the more than 10 days of learning. This program has been
promoted widely across the entire country by the Education Bureau
for cadres under the Central Organizing Committee as the model
program of the ministries and commissions under the CPC Central
Committee and the State Council. Such was the enthusiasm for the
program that some people have even called it the "Huangpu"[3] and
"Kang Da"[4] of the Ministry of Finance. This is, of course, excessive, but
it made me reflect on why it was that in the modern history of China,
the Huangpu Military Academy and the Military University of the Anti-
Japanese Invasion (Kang Da) were able to train so many elite individuals who achieved such illustrious success that comrade Mao Zedong
spoke of their "splendor" and of their "competing to be the best."
Graduates of the Huangpu Military Academy—known as "the
cradle of generals"— include Nie Rongzhen, Ye Jianying, Yun Daiying,
Chen Geng, Ying Chin and Ku Chu Tung. Kang Da graduates include
Luo Ronghuan, Lo Jui Ching, Tan Zheng and Peng Xuefeng. Indeed,
statistics show that among the first batch of generals to be commissioned
after the founding of the People's Republic of China, 90 percent were

Kang Da graduates. Could this be purely coincidental? I believe that we can distil some objective principles from these establishments.

First, the training goals were clearly defined. The Huangpu Military Academy adopted the Soviet model of training, focusing on "creating a revolutionary army to save China from its crisis." Its creed was "holding true to absolute sincerity, working together as a team, protecting the country and loving the citizens, and being unafraid to sacrifice." Kang Da focused on training its students to hold firmly to correct political directions, promoting a willingness to struggle through difficulties, and flexible military strategies and tactics.

Second, the admission of candidates was strictly controlled. The first batch of students at the Huangpu Military Academy comprised about 500 students who were carefully selected from various secondary schools and institutes of higher education from all over the country. Kang Da selected a batch of youths who, because they shared the same aspirations towards progress and revolution, were able to ensure mutual sharing and learning.

Third, there was a strong team of excellent teachers. At Huangpu, Sun Zhongshan, Chiang Kai-shek and Liao Zhongkai were, respectively, president, principal and party representative. Ye Jianying was the deputy director of the Department of Professors, and Zhou Enlai was the director of the Political Department during the third term. Many of the military instructors were graduates from the Frunze Military Academy in Russia. At Kang Da, Mao Zedong, Zhou Enlai, Liu Shaoqi and Chen Yun taught the students personally.

Fourth, there was a strong integration of academic learning and practical experience. After graduating from the Huangpu Military Academy, the graduates participated in the eastern campaign, the northern expedition and the anti-Japanese war, while Kang Da graduates went to the front line of the anti-Japanese war. It can be said that this also contributed towards their comprehensive training.

Times are different now, and there are differences in training models and local environments. The key to being effective is to stick as closely as possible to reality, looking towards the future and adapting the teaching to suit the specific requirements. While we can obtain some useful guidance from history and practical experience, we cannot simply copy these examples wholesale. We must have our own ideas, our own unique characteristics and our own creativity. Repeated investigation and research has produced the following ideas, which I would like you to think about.

Clearly-Defined Objectives

What abilities and qualities must leading accounting talents possess? This is a directional issue that we must clarify and understand. Recently I read an important paper that was jointly researched by the Shanghai National Accounting Institute and the Accounting Department—"Becoming a competent CFO—the capabilities framework of the CFO in China." It suggested that the most senior executive officers for finance and accounting in our country's enterprises should assume the following responsibilities and possess the following capabilities: Eight core functions (performance management, decision-making skills, financial strategies, provision of financial services, accounting computations and controls, provision of financial information, protection of related relationships, management responsibilities); seven core competencies (decision-making, strategic planning, analysis, leadership, collaboration, controlling ability, resource management); three core categories of abilities (vocational values, core knowledge, core skills); and 17 knowledge modules (strategic management, corporate governance, value management, acquisitions and restructuring, financial analysis, financial strategies, risk management, audit and internal controls, cost management, tax planning, financial reporting, information systems, asset management, vocational ethics, leadership of teams, communication and coordination, and systems thinking).

In my view, champions of accountancy should be high-quality and well-rounded individuals who are good in business operations, proficient in management, familiar with international practices, and have international perspectives. Apart from having rich and substantial business knowledge and foreign-language proficiency, they should also possess at least the following abilities and qualities:

First, they should possess exceptional management skills. Napoleon said, "Soldiers who do not wish to become marshals are not good soldiers." This statement may be very onerous to ordinary people, but it is extremely appropriate when applied to leading talents in accounting. If champions of accountancy are to move up the corporate ladder to take up leadership positions and the heavy responsibilities of overall management of corporate value and risk, they must possess very strong abilities to handle organizational management, communication and coordination, integrated analysis and political dealings, and to exercise professional judgment. In other words, we must not only be good generals, but must also learn to become good marshals.

Research has shown that the higher the position attained by administrative or corporate leaders, the greater is the importance of communication and coordination in their work. You must learn to sieve through all kinds of information effectively, to distinguish what is true from what is false and to extract the core essence. You must be able to observe human behavior and be proficient at communication; you must be clear with rewards and punishment, and you must be good at motivating others. If you know only how to work hard, and do not lift up your head to watch the road ahead, and are not good at handling the relationships with your superiors, your subordinates and the people around you, then you would not be qualified to lead others. The American management guru Peter Drucker said that when large-scale enterprises first emerged in the world more than 120 years ago, the only organizational institution that could provide a model for reference was the army, with its hierarchical structure, command and control, and vertical participation. However, the model for tomorrow is provided by the orchestra, soccer team and hospital, which are built around good management skills and personal judgment. How can leading accounting talents adapt to the changes in organizational management models that are brought about by globalization and information technology? This requires that management possess far-sightedness and foresight.

Second, leaders should possess a broad sphere of knowledge. The business mechanisms, scope, scale, market distribution, funding channels, organizational forms, and governance structures of the enterprises in our country are going through continual reform and development. Highly-talented accountants from businesses today not only need to deal with financial matters, they also need to deal with management policies. They need to deal with internal issues and with the various interested parties. They need to deal with key markets, both domestic and overseas. For this, they have to have broad perspectives, and be familiar with the various policies, laws and information that are related to improving the core competitiveness of the enterprise. I suggest that all of you build a series of concentric circles around your knowledge structure, where the core is accounting, and the external circles could extend to economics, management, history, literature, and so on. While I believe that one should have a thorough grasp of one field of knowledge, confining yourself to only one discipline is a huge limiting factor because you would be unable to look at problems from different perspectives. This could easily result in one-sided and biased thinking, and cause you to walk into a dead end or to split hairs over minor issues. On the other hand, mutual interaction, guidance and inspiration among different disciplines can often reap unexpected harvests, opening up completely new horizons and ways of thinking.

Third, leaders should possess strong professional ethics. Knowledge and talent provide the means, while morality and ethics provide the direction. "Those who possess both talent and ethics are saints; those who possess neither talent nor ethics are fools; people whose ethics prevail over talent are gentlemen; while people whose talent prevails over ethics are villains."[5] Of course, I'm sure none of you are fools, but you must strive to be saints (at the very least you must be gentlemen, and you must definitely not be villains). Merely having exceptional abilities is not enough; you need to have the spirit, courage and responsibility for "bearing morality on your shoulders" in order to achieve outstanding success. Without these qualities, the greater your capabilities, the higher your abilities, and the more outstanding your talents, the easier it would be to commit wrong deeds that can have disastrous consequences. A talented individual who loses moral direction is like a blind man riding a fast horse and creating danger everywhere. Accounting is fundamental to the infrastructure and workings of a market economy; the information it provides has a direct effect on the interests of investors, creditors and the general public—in short, on the economic order of the entire society. Therefore, leading accounting talents should have strong professional ethics. They should view ethics as their lifeblood, managing financial matters honestly and impartially according to the law, unaffected by power, money and popularity.

Scientific Selection

Scientifically selecting training targets with good foundations and high potential is the first step towards developing leading talents in accounting. For this purpose, we have formulated strict selection conditions and a rigorous procedure. All of you here are among the elite who have been selected through this procedure. Though I'm sure you are familiar with it, I would like remind you again of the process which brought you here.

The first stage is selecting suitable candidates. People who have senior accounting or equivalent relevant qualifications can sign up to participate in the training program. Then comes the examination segment, which is a test of the candidates' basic qualities, knowledge structures and analytical and decision-making abilities across a broad range of subjects. These include the main sections of accounting, internal corporate controls and management, and English.

Following the examination, the project working committee organizes face-to-face interviews with candidates who have obtained excellent results in the examination. This enables a further evaluation of their competence in the areas tested by the examination and provides additional information regarding such things as their analytical and linguistic abilities, adaptability, psychological quality, logical thinking, how they relate to others, as well as other areas such as self-awareness, conduct and appearance. I know that going through this series of hurdles may, for many of you, have been a form of torture, but it is only in this way that we can comprehensively evaluate and select the outstanding talent with the all-round qualities we're looking for. We are confident that through this process we are getting all the top talent from the country.

Innovative Mechanisms

"It takes talent to govern the world, and it takes education to produce talent in the world."[6] Strictly controlling the admission criteria for students is one thing, but to truly develop qualified champions of accountancy, the most important issue is how to train according to the specific needs of the students. In this regard, we need to establish a comprehensive scientific mechanism that is based on successful case studies from history; one which assimilates the essence of modern education, and which fits both the knowledge structures of the students and the objective requirements of the scheme.

First, we need innovative training mechanisms. These will not rely solely on classroom teaching but, through establishing a platform for learning, research, practice and interaction, will combine centralized training and on-the-job learning with classroom learning, research and practical experience. They will incorporate topical research, mentoring, designed reading programs, distance-learning, interactive discussion, and so on, to provide as many opportunities as possible for the students to learn, research, observe, interact and further their education, and comprehensively nurture and improve their all-round qualities.

Second, we need innovative teaching mechanisms. We need to change traditional cramming methods of teaching and establish a training concept with students as the core. The teaching plan will have to be designed around the specific needs of the students. We need to move away from the merely theoretical methods of the past and incorporate more teaching through case studies. The objective should be to improve the practical operational and research capabilities of the trainees through the interactive teaching and training of comprehensive skills using lively and effective teaching elements such as small group learning and discussions. Transforming passive learning into active learning, making full use of technologies such as online and distance teaching, will strengthen the students' interest in learning and enable the training to achieve the anticipated results.

We need to promote greater interaction and communication between students and teachers in such a way that it is not only the latter's knowledge and expertise which is passed on. We also want our students to be subconsciously influenced by their teachers and learn from their character, ethics and values. Lin Yutang said that when the students in Cambridge University met up with their mentors, the mentors would sit on their sofas, puffing away on their cigars and talking about academic subjects and about life. After a few years of such influence, the talents of the students were fully developed. Mei Yiqi, former president of Tsinghua University, also pointed out that "The school is like a pool of water, teachers and students are like fish . . . The big fish leads and the small fish follows, and over a long period of swimming together and observation, the small fish acquire the habits naturally." Therefore, "role modeling" is very important, and such unique individualized charm cannot be replicated. I hope that in this area, the training sessions can create more opportunities for students to benefit from such valuable experience.

Third, we need to establish a mechanism for incentives and restraints. This might take the form of subsidizing training and research fees for students; employing outstanding students as consultants with the Accounting Standards Committee of the Ministry of Finance and the Accounting Society of China; or enabling excellent students to participate in further education. At the same time, the introduction of an elimination system, under which only the truly outstanding who comply with the requirements can progress to a higher level of training, may motivate students to take a more active part in the training and learning.

Fourth, we need to establish a mechanism for follow-up training. For the students who participate in the training, there will be dynamic follow-up management training and, through a regular reporting and evaluation system, their learning, research and work status will be systematically recorded. We will establish a pool of highly-talented accountants and the Ministry of Finance will fully utilize the intellectual resources of the people in this pool and provide opportunities for them to display their intellectual capabilities. The structure, size and influence of the talent pool will continue to grow as more outstanding individuals are attracted to the project.

Of course, there will be expectations and requirements placed upon you, the participants, too:

First, treasure your opportunities and do not forget your responsibilities. There are more than 10 million accountants in the country, but there are only 56 people in the class today. You are the lucky ones. I hope that you will treasure this opportunity. In my view, the key factor that will determine the results of the training program is the attitude that all of you adopt towards learning. If you study seriously, you will receive a lot; if you study just to get by, you will receive very little; if you study without any sense of seriousness, you will receive nothing.

At this point, I would like to share with you my personal experience with on-the-job learning. In 2000, like all of you, I went through a long period of serious revision in preparation for a period of three and a half days of "torture." After a series of examinations in seven subjects, during which I lost four kilograms, I obtained my PhD degree at the School of Government of Peking University.

I had already passed my forty-first birthday when I started my studies. People say that you cannot learn anything after 40, but the four years of experience in striving for my PhD tell me that "going back to the furnace to be smelted again" is both necessary and very enriching. In those four years, there was tremendous growth in the depth of my knowledge and in my understanding of life. How did these changes come about? Later I was able to sum it up this way: Because of my lack of practical experience when I first attended university as a young man, I was generally unable to fully understand the theoretical knowledge that I had memorized. After graduation I engaged in practical work, and gained a wealth of social and practical experience working through a range of problems. However, I was unable to reach any generalization or enrichment at the theoretical level. The main purpose of "going back to the furnace to be smelted again" is to reflect and sum up the practical experience, learn new theories and solve the hard problems that were encountered at work. The key characteristic in this is the transformation from "learning to know" to "knowing how to learn."

In order to learn something and enrich yourself through on-the-job learning, my main experience shows that you need to grasp three things:

- that learning and work are not mutually exclusive activities; rather, they constitute a unified body. By relating to work-related thoughts during the learning process, we can deepen our understanding and accelerate the assimilation of the contents of learning;
- that learning is life. Learning is a life of high taste and high quality, and it is a self-regulatory exercise that continually improves our wisdom, and relaxes both mind and body. On-the-job learning provides a new opportunity for those who are willing to discover the real meaning of and joy in life;
- that learning is a lifetime task. Improving your personal qualities cannot be mastered very quickly and requires profound and subtle improvement over time. The ultimate test is how to improve your overall qualities and research capabilities, as well as your creativity.

Of course, on-the-job learning tests your self-control and perseverance. For example, during my PhD studies, I went through the two "furnaces"—the English examination and the written thesis—and they exhausted me mentally and physically. However, I want to assure you that the long-term rewards and enrichment you receive are well worth the price you pay on the journey. I hope that none of you has the slightest thought of relaxing your concentration. If you are to study diligently and work hard to reach the top, "always showing forth the best, and always striving to reach far ahead,"[7] you will need to strengthen your physical training and look after your health. In this way, after a few years, I believe that all of you will look back at this period of learning as an irreplaceable part of your life journey.

Second, study seriously, and expand your horizons. At previous training sessions for department heads and specialists at the Financial Systems Bureau I have stressed that learning is an honest job and that in order to truly accomplish something, to benefit and gain understanding from learning, it is necessary to be focused and to be prepared to put in some hard work. The present training session combines centralized and follow-up training. During the centralized component, which lasts for three years, we will engage first-class teachers, and arrange for everyone to carry out research and undertake practical assignments. During the two-year follow-up training, you will be allocated mentors, who will set research topics and assign certain reading and academic responsibilities to you through an interactive platform on a dedicated website. The success or failure of this training will depend on our organizational efforts and, to a large degree, on your level of participation and cooperation.

Most of you have important roles in the enterprises and are often busy in your work, particularly at the end of the year, the busiest period for the finance department. Bringing all of you together to carry out training away from your work is not easy but I hope that you will not let yourselves down or disappoint our expectations. You need to be able to handle the relationship between learning and work in such a way that they are error-free and mutually beneficial. For this, you must continue to strive to reach the top, in a spirit of eagerness and wanting to seize every moment. You will need the willpower to persevere in seemingly impossible tasks and to strengthen your learning. For this, you must cultivate good learning habits and treat learning as a requirement, a pursuit and an ideal state. You must continually acquire new knowledge and new theories; you must expand your paths and fields of learning, and learn from books, practical experience and the people around you. You must browse widely through the different fields of knowledge, and continually enrich and perfect yourself. You must, in accordance to the developments and needs of the times, combine academic theory with practical experience, striving always to apply this to the needs of the reform and opening up to the outside world and the realities of the day. You must continually increase your understanding of the relevant knowledge and improve your ability to solve problems in a focused manner.

Third, you must learn from each other and help improve each other. The 56 comrades in this training class must be one collective body and one team, and you will study together and live together for a period of time. This is a very rare opportunity for mutual interaction and learning, and I hope you will make good use of it. On the one hand, you must obey the various rules of the institute, respecting your professors and lecturers and fully displaying the highly cultivated and vigorously ambitious spirit of the leadership training program. On the other hand, you must show concern for each other, learn from each other and thus build a harmonious team that is full of vitality.

As we saw from our earlier examples of the Huangpu and Kang Da military establishments, the emergence of outstanding talent has an impact on the community. Confucius had 3,000 disciples under him and 72 sages; the "Manhattan Project" implemented in the United States produced a large batch of top scientists including Robert Oppenheimer, Enrico Fermi, Moddie Taylor, Arthur Compton, and Ernest Lawrence. Harvard University has produced six presidents, dozens of famous scientists and writers and 32 Nobel Prize winners; more than two-thirds of its graduates have gone on to occupy important positions as senior members of the cabinet and high court judges. One very important factor is that when a group of outstanding individuals walk together, they can discuss, interact and improve each other. This is what education is about. Henry Rosovsky, former Dean of the Faculty of Arts and Sciences at Harvard University, once remarked that he'd often heard people say that students learn more from each other than they learn directly from the teachers.

Individually and collectively, you represent a treasure trove of expertise and rich experience. I hope that you will contribute your respective ideas, experiences and wisdom to enrich and enlighten each other.

Dear comrades, the learning time during the training sessions is but a short path along the road of life, but I believe that it will come to occupy a big part of your memories. There is a saying that "even when we grow old and our hair becomes white, we still seem to be strangers." This seems to refer to our general failure to connect on an emotional level, even with people and places we may have known for many years. There are, however, some people and some places which cause you to fall in love at first sight and with which you develop an intense sense of connection that continues for a lifetime. I believe that you will form just such a lifetime's attachment to the Shanghai National Accounting Institute and to your classmates with whom you share this intense but joyful time.

ENDNOTES

1 This is an edited version of the speech given at the Inaugural Ceremony for the Senior Accounting Talent Training Program, December 10, 2005. The

title is based on a quote from Yang Jisheng, a scholar of the Ming Dynasty, and revised by Li Dazhao, a Chinese intellectual and one of the founders of the Chinese Communist Party.

2 "Two standards" refers to the *Accounting Standards for Business Enterprises* and *Financial Standards for Business Enterprises*. "Two systems" refers to the accounting system for business enterprises for 13 industries and the financial system for business enterprises for 10 industries, which were put into effect on July 1, 1993, putting an end to the accounting model of the planned economy.

3 Officially opened on June 16, 1924, the Whampoa Military Academy was a military academy in the Republic of China (ROC) that produced many prestigious commanders who fought in many of China's conflicts in the 20th century, including the Anti-Japanese War (1937–1945).

4 It was founded in June 1936. Like Whampoa Military Academy, the college produced many commanders who fought in the Anti-Japanese War.

5 From *Zizhi Tongjian* (Comprehensive Mirror to Aid in Government), a pioneering reference work in Chinese historiography, published in 1084. The book, in 294 volumes, narrates chronologically the history of China from the Warring States to the Five Dynasties (403 BC–959 CE). The major contributor was Sima Guang.

6 A quote from Hu Yuan (993–1059), a famous educator in the Song Dynasty.

7 Quoted from a poem by Cui Yan (1058–1126), an official of the Song Dynasty.

Chapter 3

Making Your Writings More Citable and Your Students More Useful to Society[1]

As the first concentration training for the inaugural National Accountancy Prospective Academic Leaders Training Program comes to a smooth conclusion, on behalf of the Party Leadership Group of the Ministry of Finance and Minister Jin Renqing, I sincerely extend warm congratulations to all those among you who have been selected to be leading academic talents in accounting. I would also like to express our heartfelt thanks for the attention and support given by the Xiamen National Accounting Institute.

All of you are experts in research into accounting theories, and already have recorded achievements in many areas. Your selection for the training program for leading academic talents in accounting is a full affirmation of your many years of diligent studies and conscientious work, and a form of motivation for you to strive for further progress. During this period of training, all of you will have gained greater insight and understanding, and I would like to share a few opinions and thoughts regarding the issues related to the training of outstanding accounting academics.

I'd like to begin with the question: What is a leading talent? I'm sure we've all seen the V-shaped formations of geese in flight. A leading academic talent is like the goose which flies in front of the formation, providing the direction, acting as a role model for the others to follow. Practical experience has proven that an outstanding leading academic is always able to develop a team of academic researchers capable of creating major breakthroughs in their respective fields of research. What qualities should leading academic talents in accounting possess and how should these qualities be cultivated in our training program? In my view, this new generation of leading academic talents must have virtues, abilities and practical achievements. These three areas are linked and indispensable.

Cultivating virtues should be the first priority. As expressed in *Shuo Wen Jie Zi*[2] "virtues come from an upright heart." The explanation given in the *Annotations of the Analects of Confucius* is that "virtues mean self-realization" and "our actions result from the virtues that are cultivated in our hearts." Subsequently, this has been extended to incorporate moral cultivation and ideological quality, working attitudes and working styles, self-awareness and disciplinary concepts. When we say that leading academics in accounting have "virtues," it means that they maintain the values of integrity and fairness and liberal progress.

Market economics rely on the "invisible hand" to realize the optimal allocation of assets, and morality is a basic condition for the successful operation of the market mechanism. Adam Smith wrote *The Wealth of Nations* and *The Theory of Moral Sentiments*, in which he expounded the important function of morality in the process of economic growth. Academic anomalies and misconduct are the result of improper academic morals. Among the ranks of academic cheats can be found alumni of prestigious schools, seemingly reputable teachers and overseas returnees. Some even assume leadership roles in institutions or in society. Yet such people lack the character qualities that are essential in true leaders.

As leading academics in accounting, how can we achieve the state of being "virtuous"? I believe that we need to practise the "Eight Dos and Eight Don'ts" from the socialist moral norms of honor and disgrace.[3] At the same time, we need to integrate these practices into the accountancy profession, to forge and promote the spirit of accounting in China.

First, we must be honest and trustworthy: Pan Xulun, the father of modern accounting in China, pointed out that trust is the lifeblood of accounting work: "Without trust, there will be no accounting." International Federation of Accountants President Graham Ward, during the 2009 Release Ceremony on Chinese Accounting Standards for Business Enterprises and Auditing Standards, pointed out that trust, professionalism and transparency are significant characteristics that differentiate the accountancy profession from other industries. Academic leaders in accounting must always remember and cultivate the spirit of trustworthiness that is manifested in the motto of the Lixin Accounting Institute: "demonstrating trust when making resolutions, demonstrating trust for self-preservation, demonstrating trust when dealing with society, demonstrating trust when dealing with others, never forgetting to establish trust, and demonstrating absolute sincerity."[4]

Second, we must be objective and fair: The accounting profession bears the responsibility for protecting the interests of the general public and promotes the comprehensive coordination of the sustainable development of the economy and society. Establishing a sense of objectivity and fairness is both an internal requirement of professional ethics in accounting and an objective requirement for the accounting function to be fully developed. To uphold the spirit of objectivity and fairness, academic leaders in accounting must be impartial in seeking the truth based on facts.

Third, we must keep an open mind: Currently, following the rapid progress of globalization and the rapid growth of the economy in our country, the economic activities that confront the accountancy profession are becoming more rigorous and varied, and the relevant theories more diverse. This requires that accounting personnel, particularly leading academic talent, possess a broad vision and open minds in applying the lessons learned at home and abroad, integrating domestic and foreign accounting, economic and management theories to promote major developments in academic research.

Fourth, we must continually strive for further progress and innovation: The world is progressing, and the accounting field is being enriched. Academic leaders in accounting should therefore cultivate their personal sense of striving and the spirit of innovation, adapting to new scenarios, exploring new ideas, solving new problems and continually promoting innovation and theoretical improvements.

The emphasis should be on abilities. "Abilities" refer to talents, which relates to the capacity to serve society. When we say that leading academics in accounting should have abilities, it means that they should possess a wealth of knowledge, a high level of professionalism and outstanding organizational management capabilities.

First, the candidate must possess outstanding academic abilities: These include the ability to observe issues—the starting point for any kind of theoretical research—without which it is impossible to identify the problems that exist in a specific area of research. True observation is a combination of observation and analysis, the second of the essential academic abilities. It is only through the strict application of logical reasoning and accurate empirical analysis that the scientific nature of the research process can be strengthened to produce reliable conclusions. The third area is innovative ability—the spirit of independent creativity that can highlight previously undiscovered or unconsidered perspectives and thus make a substantial contribution to the accumulation of academic knowledge.

Second, the candidate must possess a comprehensive knowledge structure: John Maynard Keynes pointed out that "qualified economists must be endowed with a combination of many talents." Leading academics in accounting, too, must also possess a combination of specialized and general abilities, of specialized and broad-based understanding. They must have a firm grasp of the theoretical knowledge and practical skills that underpin the accounting profession but they should also be familiar with related fields and disciplines such as economics, management and law. This requires them to be proficient in the theories of the humanities and social sciences, and have an understanding of the natural sciences. Possessing this kind of knowledge structure enables leading academic talents to develop concentric circles in accounting theory.

Third, the candidate should possess outstanding organizational management ability: Having completed the training program, many of you will move quickly into leadership positions which will require strong organizational management abilities, the ability to communicate clearly and the ability to grasp and analyze policies and make professional judgments based on that analysis. You will also need to be proficient in planning strategies, working with your team to carry out specific teaching and scientific research work that will promote the development of the accounting profession.

The end-result should be practical achievements. The final goal in the Ministry of Finance's talent-cultivation strategy is to lead the virtues and talents of senior accounting talent towards practical applications that can contribute towards the growth of the economy and society. There are numerous routes to this end.

First, make your articles more widely citable by other people. As you are all doctors, associate professors or professors, it should not be difficult for you to write articles for publication. However, quality is more important than quantity. Only quantity which is regulated by quality will have any significance. A document which has no substance or is merely repeating the viewpoints of other people is unable to leave behind any legacy for the academic field. The crucial test for an article is whether its ideological viewpoints, core contents and innovative concepts gain wide acceptance and can be used by other academics. This is a high standard. When your article is published, it is subjected to close scrutiny from your peers. If it is a good article, people take notice, use it and disseminate it. Generally speaking, excellent scientific research results are able to exercise fairly widespread influence on society. An innovative academic viewpoint or a valuable academic finding would have a higher rate of usage and would receive more positive evaluation.

Second, make your students useful to society. "A teacher passes on knowledge, educates on various subjects, and solves problems."[5] As leading academics in accounting, it is your responsibility to impart your knowledge through lectures as well as through being a role model in your life and work. My hope is that you dedicate yourselves fully to developing high-quality all-round talent whose effect will be felt throughout the accounting field and in the wider domain of economic research. If you can do this, you will have attained outstanding practical achievements. I hope that in the future your students will feel a sense of pride and honor that they had you as their teacher. Enable your students to play greater roles in society, and allow the legacy of your academic wisdom to be passed on and developed further through the lives of your students.

Third, let your accomplishments influence the fields outside of accounting. The various disciplines which make up what we call the social sciences did not come about naturally, and the classification and re-classification of the disciplines can be seen in a certain sense to be for the purpose of facilitating research. Accounting was initially a sub-discipline within the study of management, and, by association, of economics and social studies. Therefore, reinforcing the connections between the study of accounting and other related academic disciplines for the purposes of cross-disciplinary research is an important mission for every leading academic talent and an important indicator for evaluating your qualifications to be a leader.

Fourth, let your name have a greater measure of influence on future generations of academics. To be a leading academic in accounting, it is not enough to establish a reputation or produce some accomplishments in a certain time and at a certain place. Only when your name is remembered by future generations of academics and your work continues to have an impact on future generations of academics can it be said that you are a true leading academic talent, and that you have truly succeeded.

While this training program guides people towards becoming leaders, whether you have the perseverance and diligence necessary to take it further and develop your full potential is entirely up to you. As we have seen, apart from acquiring an extensive database of knowledge through extensive reading, you will also need to take on major responsibilities, gain practical experience, and maintain a spirit of exploration and a creative passion.

A leading academic in accounting is not just an honorary title; it also represents a character model and carries considerable responsibility. This could be burdensome but it could also be a source of power to propel you forward throughout your life. Each individual should learn to enjoy the sense of enrichment and achievement that is found in work, as well as the sweetness and relaxation that are found in life. However, since you possess the potential, qualities and abilities, and have been chosen for this task, you should embrace the responsibility of enhancing accounting research in China. The path you have chosen will require that you work harder and face greater pressures than your peers. Whether you are giving lectures, writing articles or teaching students, you will need a sense of responsibility and a sense of mission. From now onwards, you must cultivate a sense of leadership, and assume the responsibilities that go with your chosen career.

As Albert Einstein pointed out, "Identifying a problem is often more important than solving a problem. True progress in science requires problems to be identified, particularly the identification of difficult problems." You need to observe the world closely and look for topical issues which will allow you to think always about how to write more creatively, express more clearly, and describe more profoundly. It is from the collision of ideas that new academic viewpoints and understanding arise. My experience is that when the mind thinks through a few topical issues at the same time or from different angles, this exercise helps to integrate knowledge and aid comparative research. This can definitely help in resolving at least one of the problems to get good results.

All the events we encounter, the people we meet and the books we read will be related to our research, and you need to be open to the possibility that they can supplement, contribute towards, inspire, renew or improve your original way of thinking, writing and understanding. Allow me to relate to you a personal experience of how such associative thinking can work to your benefit.

While I was dealing with a problem of driving forward the project to converge Chinese accounting standards with international standards, friends from the International Accounting Standards Board (IASB) would often speak about fair-value accounting, insisting that convergence with international standards would entail a complete copying of those standards. Despite my best efforts, I could do nothing to persuade them otherwise. Just as I was finding it hard to think of a solution, I heard a radio program about the APEC organization, which essentially said that APEC is not a mandatory organization with binding force at the administrative, legal or moral level, but is merely a consultative organization. It suddenly dawned on me that the IASB does not have the power to bind us at the administrative, legal or moral level either. This prompted me to think about what we needed to do to gain a common understanding. I began to see that it would require consultation and compromise—"You give a little ground to me, I give a little ground to you; you take some initiative, I take some initiative"—to enable both parties to move closer to finding a solution. With this inspiration, I proposed a set of principles for promoting convergence which saw convergence as a process and a form of mutual interaction, rather than as a simple, direct copying of the standards. IASB's chairman Sir David Tweedie[6] accepted my viewpoint willingly.

I believe the same applies in the academic field. If your mind is open to forming associations between the events that you encounter, and you consciously extract and process the relevant portions and consolidate these to become part of your own knowledge, ideas, viewpoints and discourse, it is possible to learn a subject well. "Our lives are limited, while knowledge is limitless."[7] There are so many different academic disciplines that it is impossible to learn everything. However, if you are proficient at absorbing knowledge from the various disciplines and know how to carry out associative thinking, this will undoubtedly benefit your academic pursuits. The byways of academic study can quickly become the main stream.

Many things require continual and repeated re-thinking. We need to think hard about things, questioning and answering, answering and rebutting, rebutting and reflecting. For this, we need to empty ourselves, so that our spirit can be serene and clear. It is only in this way that we can understand or get close to the core of things, and achieve a deep state whereby knowledge is extended. I believe that if a person does not have a thinking process like Bodhidharma's utter devotion to contemplation, going the extra mile and exploring all possibilities, there will be many viewpoints that will not be understood. Such understanding is not a simple sum derived from addition, a product derived from multiplication, a quotient derived from division or a difference derived from subtraction. It may be a composite index, a transformation built around a fusion of ideas, viewpoints, knowledge and experience.

Without a rigorous thinking process, there can be no elevation in understanding. The famous scientist Professor Tsung-Dao Lee's theory of the "connection between science and art" is a model example of deep thinking and scientific understanding. From the artist Huang Zhou's drawing of a donkey, he came to understand the enormous energy in nuclear power, and from the ancient poet Qu Yuan's *Tian Wen*, he came to understand the theories of astronomy. Deep contemplation is a lifelong process, and we need to persevere with it. Deep contemplation requires that we think as deeply and broadly as possible to discover connections and draw inspiration from seemingly unconnected things. Discovery, moments of inspiration, can come in the most unexpected of places: While in bed, on a horse or in the bathroom. This feeling of "turning around by chance and seeing that what we seek is right there where the lights were waning"[8] and the sense of "elation of discovering what you are seeking for after a long process of seeking"[9] are actually the results from a flash of insight after deep contemplation, and have an effect similar to "the fragrance of the plum blossom coming from the bitter cold."[10]

DILIGENT REMINDERS AND CONSTANT CORRECTIONS

Not everyone has a good memory. Even if you do, it is certainly better to write things down. It is only by recording something and continually editing, correcting and improving it, that we can finally form a masterpiece in the end. The Russian writer Gogol took his pen and notebook with him wherever he went. If he heard any interesting anecdotes or aphorisms, he noted them down for later use in his essays. This is something that I would recommend to you all. When you see or hear something interesting, or you have an idea, write it down immediately. Don't put it off or make excuses. If you leave things till later, the moment and the spark of inspiration may have passed. Inspiration is like a shooting star; and if you don't capture that fleeting moment of brilliance, it may not come again. If your memory is good, you may still be able to recall most of what you thought about in the night when you wake in the morning. If so, I would advise you to make this your first priority when you wake up. If you do not do this, you may not be able to remember the details when you need them later, which can be very frustrating. If you do not feel frustrated in such circumstances, then I would advise you not to be a researcher in the theoretical field.

A good article is one which has been edited well. This needs to be a continuous process because man's understanding is continually changing according to time, locations and circumstance. For example, in 1867 the US Secretary of State William Seward purchased Alaska from Russia for US\$7.2 million. At the time, the Russians thought they had gained a windfall, while the Americans were very dissatisfied with the transaction, which they often ridiculed as "Seward's Ice Box" or "Seward's Folly." This was because Alaska appeared to be completely useless: It was far away from American soil, making administration and logistics difficult; and the land value was small. However, circumstances changed: First, gold was discovered there, then oil and, later, substantial coal reserves. Subsequently, it was further discovered that the land had ecological attractions that were priceless and its geographical location had strategic military significance, which obviously upset the Russians a great deal.

We need to be always aware that people's perceptions change with time and circumstance, and constantly work to revise and improve our reasoning in line with developments and changes. For example, after you have taken notes from a lecture, gained some insights from an article you have read or a meeting you have attended, or heard a child make an innocent remark which is full of philosophical truth, you should at all times supplement, edit and improve the article you are formulating or the issue you are researching.

In striving to become leading academic talents, we must be keen to listen to different opinions, particularly those of the experts, and make use of the ideological collisions to promote our understanding to a higher level. For example, when Liang Qichao—who passed the imperial examination at the age of 18 and thought of himself as an erudite scholar—heard a lecture by Kang Youwei in Guangdong, he felt as if he had heard "the lion's roar and the sound of the ocean tides," and it dawned upon him at that moment that his understanding was shallow. He therefore humbly acknowledged Kang Youwei as his teacher. If it had not been for this "wake-up call" the world might have lost an erudite reformer.

It is written in the *Book of Rites—Record on the Subject of Education*[11] that "learning in isolation will lead to shallow understanding." If our understanding is to grow, we need to interact with the masters and experts who have walked a similar path and can show us how to avoid detours and thus shorten the process. The use of role models is a long-established tradition in Chinese culture. Confucius, for example, trained many successful disciples, who came to be known as the "3,000 disciples and 72 sages." These disciples experienced trials, hardship and joy along with him and it was this experience that helped them to organize and edit the *Analects*, which captured the incisive words, vivid demeanor and profound philosophies of their teacher. This was not something that could be done by simply attending a single lecture, but was the result of subtle influence through long-term interaction and the meeting of minds.

But I am not advocating here that you live in some academic ivory tower. We also need to engage with everyday events in the real world and, through our practical experience, increase our talents and nurture our abilities. This is even more important if we are dealing with application-based research or research on practical operations.

TAKING A BIRD'S-EYE VIEW AND CHECKING THE REAR VIEW

No matter what research we are engaged in, we need to adopt an overarching, strategic perspective. We need to step outside and above immediate circumstances to get an overall view, rather than taking the risk of getting caught up in the fine details and thus of going around in ever-decreasing circles so that we can't see the wood for the trees. For us, this entails stepping out of the accounting field, and carrying out our research from a multi-disciplinary perspective and with a global vision. For example, when we analyze the problems related to accounting in China, which is still a developing nation in transition, if we view things from a global perspective, it is more likely to stimulate new ideas, new concepts and new methods.

Apart from taking a bird's-eye view of things, I would also encourage you to look back. For example, when you're driving a car, obviously you have to look to the front, but you must also learn how to use the rear-view mirror, and see whether other people are going to overtake you and whether it's safe to make a turn. When you are dealing with academic research, you need to lead others, but you must also be aware of what's going on around you to help you determine the advantages and disadvantages in your research methods. Sometimes you need to pull back a little to adjust, improve, and enhance your approach. A boxer generates more power in a punch by first pulling his fist back, and it is the same with ideas.

INDEPENDENT INNOVATION

Chinese people are very intelligent, and Chinese children often rank first or second in their class when they are studying overseas. However, no one from China has ever won a Nobel Prize. Why is this? One of the reasons is that our creativity and imagination have not been fully unleashed. The CPC Central Committee is currently advocating that we dedicate our efforts towards building an innovation-based country, which presents a golden opportunity for people engaged in scientific research. The entire society is promoting and encouraging innovation; and in such a good climate, the crucial factor is your personal diligence.

There is a view that says that first-class academics create knowledge, while third-class academics transmit knowledge, and there is a lot of truth in this statement. An academic who remains at the level of the gramophone and photocopier, simply re-packaging and repeating the viewpoints of his predecessors, is destined to have a very limited academic lifespan. It has been suggested that it would save us a lot of time and effort if we simply dealt with the practical aspects of accounting, leaving the theoretical research to foreign academics. In my view, however, if we simply import theories generated under different economic environments and economic models, and pay no attention to independent innovation at the theoretical level or to the specific needs of economic reform and development in our country, this would only widen the gap between our accountancy profession and those of other advanced nations.

Therefore, carrying out research and scholarly pursuits cannot be a mechanical repetition or a blind going with the flow. Since you have all chosen the path of research, it is your responsibility to come up with new ideas, new concepts and new methods. As a leading academic talent, you must have an independent spirit, be liberal in your thinking and be boldly innovative. Chen Yinke once cautioned future generations of scholars that "a scholar who engages in scholarly learning must break the shackles of the common truth from his aspirations," and praised Wang Guowei's "independence of spirit [and] freedom of thought, which will shine brightly forever." You too must have such independence of spirit and the courage to bring innovations, throwing away the impulse to make quick gains or to rely on blind copying. Using advanced accounting theories from overseas as a reference for your work in accordance with the actual requirements of our country's economic development, you can continually improve your research methods, strengthen theoretical innovation and advance the development of accounting theories.

MAINTAINING YOUR PASSION

Where there is no passion, there will be no creativity. No matter what task we are performing, if there is no passion that springs up from within you and a dedication that "leaves no room for regrets,"[12] or if there is only a pursuit of fame and riches, then even though you may achieve some small measure of success in your career, you will definitely not reach the pinnacle. If you "write books only for the sake of making a living"[13] or if you go around giving lectures in the hope of gaining fame and riches, then your creativity will be mediocre and your output anemic and shallow. You will never achieve the unmatched quality that creates awe and enlightens our thinking.

Famous musical or literary works that are passed down through generations are largely the result of passion. For example, the famous *Blue Danube* by Johann Strauss and the concertos by Chopin, which have been described as "music of the heart that emerges only when first love is present," are both classics in the world of music; Yue Fei's *Man Jiang Hong* (*The River All Red*) that is widely read in China and Fang Zhimin's *Adorable China* that has inspired countless martyrs are classics in the literary field. In your research on accounting theories, you must incorporate passion into the work, and allow your life to flow within the scholarly erudition, and your dedication to be manifest within the articles you write.

However, passion requires a lot of energy, and intellectual and physical effort. The famous writer Lu Yao once said that writing requires both intellectual and physical effort. Once you enter the creative state, it is like entering a vast expanse of marshes, where there is no village ahead and no shop behind; it is like running a lonely marathon. I feel deeply about this point, and regardless of whether it is writing a manuscript, handling systems or formulating policies, it is a very difficult job. Sometimes when draft documents have to be produced in a hurry, mealtimes are forgotten as you burn the midnight oil to finish the work.

As a leading academic talent, you will be required to endure hardship, and to do so with pride and joy. You will not see the rainbow unless you have gone through the storm. If passion is the storm that erupts from deep within your soul, then after the storm passes, you would feel a sense of spiritual quietness and peace. When I was working in an accounting firm, I had an old comrade (who was also my teacher) who, every time he finished an official document or draft manuscript, would sing *Xi Pi Liu Shui* along the corridor and hum a tune that was comprehensible only to himself. Everyone, including myself, was deeply infected with the sense of joy that came from the harvest following hard labor. Such joy can only be experienced by talented people who are filled with passion in working to complete the task at hand.

HOW TO NURTURE LEADERS

"It takes talent to govern the world, and it takes education to produce talent in the world."[14] How we select and nurture leading academics in accounting will determine the success and failure of the project to raise accounting standards. I would like to share with you here some of my ideas and understanding of the matter.

Examinations are an important route for selecting talent and promoting movement within and across the various levels of society.

Whether it is today's college examinations or the civil servant recruitment system, or the imperial examinations of ancient times, they have all made important contributions. Although not perfect, examinations are nonetheless our best method at this present moment. It is essential to guarantee the universality, fairness and scientific nature of the examinations.

In order for the training program for leading academics in accounting to nurture leaders, it is vital that the selection process is managed well, to ensure that only the best candidates—with the correct professional foundations, all-round qualities and high development potential—are selected. For this purpose, we have formulated strict selection criteria and procedures. As you all know from your own experience, only candidates holding the rank of doctor, associate professor and above are eligible for consideration. The written section of the selection process tests the theoretical foundations, analytical abilities and problem-solving skills of the candidates across a wide range of professional subjects, including accounting, financial management and audit. The written examination also has an English-language component which includes English–Chinese translation and analysis of the English language. Those who pass the written examination then undergo an oral interview which provides a comprehensive evaluation of each candidate's research ability, knowledge structure and linguistic expression. The interview also reveals the candidates' ability to evaluate and analyze, to organize and coordinate, their adaptability, their psychological qualities, their reasoning ability, and their conduct and appearance.

It is only through comprehensive, strict and scientific considerations that we can actually select outstanding talent with the necessary qualities.

LIBERAL EDUCATION

The sayings "When we live among good people, we will naturally be upright" and "We will be influenced for the good if we stick around good people, and we will be influenced for the bad if we stick around bad people" teach us the importance of a good environment. This leads to the question of how we can further improve the external environment for nurturing leading academic talents and promote the rapid growth of senior accounting talent. I believe that the crucial factor in this is the liberalization of education.

Last year I attended a week of classes at the London Business School, which made a deep impression on me. Both the lecturers and the students were at a senior level, and came from different parts of the world. Everyone had different knowledge backgrounds, ideological viewpoints and visions and experiences, and used the latest theories in their respective fields to investigate and analyze problems. This interaction resulted in a convergence of knowledge, vision and viewpoints, and an expansion of thinking. When they talked about issues related to China, or to the United States, or to Europe, or to Africa, or to emerging markets, they knew the subject like the back of their hand; it was like talking about the issues in their own backyards. Therefore, liberal education is very important. In order to realize liberal education, the crucial factor is to build a broad platform that enables students to interact deeply with their teachers and fellow students, with experts—domestic and foreign—from the same profession and from other fields, and with successful people outside academia.

First, strengthen the interaction between teachers and students. We need to promote greater communication between students and teachers in such a way that the students gain knowledge and are subconsciously influenced by the character, ethics and values of the teacher.

Second, strengthen the interaction among students. All of you here have been selected via a rigorous selection process, which proves that you have a solid theoretical background and great potential to develop further. You must look on each of your fellow students as a treasure trove of ideas, experiences and wisdom that can help you consolidate and contribute what you know. Each of you can be enlightened and enriched by others. You need to come together more often to drink coffee and bounce ideas off each other. In future centralized trainings we will reserve some time for you to have opportunities to enlighten, interact with and enrich each other.

In the near future, programs similar to this will be held for enterprise, CPA and administrative unit leaders. While the students from these other programs will have had considerable experience in the practical work departments, their theoretical background still has some room for improvement. The academic qualifications of the students in our program are, as you know, very high, and you have a clear advantage in the theoretical aspects of the profession. However, you lack practical working experience. Interaction and cooperation among the training programs will be strengthened to enable all participants to learn from each other. Perhaps some of you will go to give lectures at the training program for enterprise leaders so that there can be an exchange of experiences.

We will also work to strengthen the interaction with the various sectors in society, including the various levels of government accounting agencies and other fields in economics and management. We are arranging with other universities for you to attend their executive MBA classes to interact with CEOs from multinational corporations in Japan, Korea and China. At the same time, we are arranging for outstanding students to participate in related academic interaction with the Ministry of Finance, the Accounting Society of China and the National Accounting Institute.

As part of our push to promote the internationalization strategy for leading academics in accounting, we need to learn and import advanced research methods and concepts from overseas. We also need to take China's unique accounting theories to the international forum to expand the influence of our country's academic talent and promote greater understanding of our systems in the international community.

STRENGTHEN MANAGEMENT

The training and talent-development methods we use must reflect and be adapted to the differences and diversity found among the prospective leaders who are selected for our programs. Training should be conducted in accordance with the students' abilities and should be made to measure, so as to accelerate the growth of talent. This can be done in a number of ways.

Firstly, the training concept must have students at its core and must focus on their individual requirements. We must increase the proportion of teaching through case studies with a view to improving the students' practical operational and research capabilities. Interactive teaching and training of comprehensive skills should incorporate small-group learning, group discussions and outreach training, making full use of available technologies such as online and long-distance teaching to provide the students with a convenient platform for interaction.

Training and subject fees can be subsidized to encourage participation. A scientific recording and appraisal system of the students' research subjects, theses and published works will focus on quality rather than quantity. This will make it easier to assess whether new problems, materials or data are being uncovered and whether new viewpoints, methods or theories are being proposed to deal with them. It will also make it easier to determine the quality of research being undertaken and which students are meeting the criteria for entry into the next cycle of higher-level training. Students who fail to meet the requirements of the appraisal indicators should be released from the program. This may seem harsh but, seen from the perspective of the entire group, it is scientific and fair.

Topical research and training must be strengthened, and academic research capabilities must be further enhanced. Every student must assume responsibility for ensuring that their research topics are integrated with the core tasks of the Ministry of Finance, such as research on internal controls for accounting in the enterprises, or with their personal practical work, and connected to the State's key funding projects.

It is important, too, to establish a system for announcing the results of the appraisal and for providing feedback. This will serve to actively encourage and support the students to produce more and better results. At the same time, it is also important to provide funding for results that can be swiftly transformed into production capabilities.

All students who participate in the training enter the talent pool, where the intellectual resources and skills of those who produce the necessary results will be fully utilized by the Ministry of Finance in formulating national accounting reform and development policies. The talent pool will be subject to dynamic management such that it will be continuously refreshed and enriched with outstanding new talent and ideas.

The first concentration training for prospective leading academics in accounting is only the first step on a long and arduous journey. I hope that all of you will remember the responsibility that comes with this honor and will use it as motivation as you undertake the historical mission on your shoulders. It is my hope that, through mutual interaction and continual engagement, each of you will improve and cultivate your personal abilities to establish a sense of leadership, innovation and progress. Through diligent learning and deep research, may each of you unearth and fulfill your potential, working hard together to usher in a flourishing period of growth for accounting theories in China and display the nation's strengths in the accounting field on the international stage.

ENDNOTES

1 Edited version of a speech given at the National Accountancy Prospective Academic Leaders Training Program, April 22, 2006.

2 *Shuo Wen Jie Zi* ("Explaining Simple and Analyzing Compound Characters") was an early second-century Chinese dictionary from the Han Dynasty. Its author was Xu Shen (58–147 CE), a Chinese philologist of the Han Dynasty. It contains over 9,000 character entries explaining the origins of the characters based primarily upon a study of the earlier seal script. It was the first Chinese dictionary to analyze the structure and rationale of the characters.

3 The *Ba Rong Ba Chi* (Eight Honours and Eight Shames), officially the Core Value System or the Eight Honours and Disgraces, is a set of moral concepts developed by current President Hu Jintao for the citizens of the People's Republic of China. Its formal name in China is "Socialist Concepts on Honors and Disgraces." The English translation of the details posted by the Xinhua News Agency in October 2006 are:

> *Love the country; do it no harm.*
> *Serve the people; never betray them.*
> *Follow science; discard superstition.*
> *Be diligent; not indolent.*
> *Be united, help each other; make no gains at others' expense.*
> *Be honest and trustworthy; do not sacrifice ethics for profit.*
> *Be disciplined and law-abiding; not chaotic and lawless.*
> *Live plainly, work hard; do not wallow in luxuries and pleasures.*

4 The Lixin Accounting Institute was founded by Pan Xulun (1893–1985), an outstanding Chinese accountant and educator.

5 From *On Teachers* by Han Yu (768–824), a famous essayist and poet of the Tang dynasty who is listed among the "Eight Great Prose Masters of the Tang and Song."

6 Chairman of the International Accounting Standards Board.

7 From Zhuang Zi, an influential Chinese philosopher who lived around the fourth century BCE during the Warring States Period, corresponding to the Hundred Schools of Thought philosophical summit of Chinese thought.

8 A famous and often-cited line from a poem by Xin Qiji (1140–1207), one the greatest composers of the Ci form of poetry.

9 From a poem by Jia Dao (779–843), a poet of the Tang Dynasty.

10 A popular and frequently cited aphorism in China.

11 One of the Five Classics of the Confucian canon, it describes the social forms, government system, and ancient/ceremonial rites of the Zhou Dynasty (c.1050–256 BCE). The original text is believed to have been compiled by Confucius himself, while the copy society refers to now has been edited and re-worked by various scholars of the Han Dynasty (202 BCE–220 CE).

12 A line from a poem by Liu Yong (987–1053), a Ci poet in the Song Dynasty.

13 From a poem of Gong Zizhen (1792–1841), a writer and thinker of the Qing Dynasty.

14 A quote from Hu Yuan (993–1059), a famous educator in the Song Dynasty.

Honesty is the Core of Integrity; Awakening is the Prerequisite to Achievement[1]

TAKING STOCK AND RAISING AWARENESS

The Chinese philosopher Mozi once said: "A country will be well run and strong when wise and benevolent administrators are plentiful. Where the latter are scarce, the country will be in disarray and weak." In the accountancy profession, the development of talented individuals is a decisive factor in the rise of the whole profession. Whoever excels in building a talented team is certain to be in a commanding position in the competitive international business market. Any accounting practitioner who is ambitious and conscientious—whether he is some-one who manages the development of the profession or a practitioner in an accounting practice—should recognize the need to develop talent through training.

A nation's development is dependent on the quality and quantity of the talent at its disposal. This is true in whatever place or period of history you care to look. While there can be no doubting the fact that

China is bestowed with an abundance of talent, it is equally true that we lack experienced senior professionals. Statistics show that only 5.5 percent of all practitioners are professionals in the strictest sense, which is less than one-quarter of the proportion in developed countries. Therefore, China's prime strategy at this stage of its social and economic development is focused on the nurturing of professional talent. We need a large number of creative and adventurous individuals who are able to meet the challenges presented by modern technological development, to build a harmonious socialist society and to boost our competitiveness. Strengthening the accounting profession, especially its leadership, constitutes an important step forward in this respect.

Faced with the challenges brought by globalization and the pragmatic needs of the development of our economy, China has increased and broadened its participation and cooperation in projects with other countries while, at the same time, intensifying and widening the areas in which it competes with them. As the market for accounting has opened up, China's accounting firms are now subjected to ever-increasing competition from other countries. Apart from improving our accounting practices and the regulatory regime of the market to provide a level playing field for everyone, we can further strengthen the profession by accelerating the pace of the development of talented individuals within it. Meanwhile, we are faced with an important issue of how Chinese certified public accountants, with their specific professional edge and international perspective, can help Chinese companies enter the international accounting market. We must recognize the need to train our talented people to international standards to raise the standards within our country and to compete with others in the international arena.

Much progress has been made in the development of our profession and much has been achieved in training since the rebuilding of the CPA profession. While big strides have been taken in improving the quality of our accountants, the profession as a whole still suffers from inconsistency in standards. In particular, we do not have enough quality certified public accountants who meet the challenges of high-level competition. If we are unable to address this problem soon, we run the risk of losing out to our international peers in competing for the many opportunities that globalization brings. Providing suitable training has become a matter of urgency and is a mammoth task in itself.

Among the major objectives for our profession over the next five years, as presented by Minister Jin Renqing at the fourth National Congress of the Chinese Institute of Certified Public Accountants (CICPA), is one to build an army of practitioners who are capable in both numbers and the ability to meet the challenges brought by China's economic development. With this in mind, and after conducting in-depth analysis and research into the current state of the profession, the CICPA published its *30 Guiding Opinions on Reinforcing Cultivation of Professional Talents* in June 2005 (hereafter referred to as the *30 Opinions*), which establish the guiding philosophy, general rationale and specific measures in developing talented certified public accountants.

The *30 Opinions* have distilled the wisdom and embodied the wishes of our profession and are an important compass in guiding the initiation of our talent-building exercise. Everyone in our profession takes the full implementation of the *30 Opinions* very seriously and strives to put each and every principle and measure fully into practice.

To date, the CICPA has run a successful overseas training course in accounting practices for senior management executives and also launched the *Overseas Internship Project for Students Majoring in CPA*. It has held English exams and comprehensive aptitude tests, and so on. The initial outcomes of the implementation of the *30 Opinions* were clear and there is now a pool of experience from which we can draw.

What we need to do next is to build on these foundations to establish a framework with a designated leadership-development focus and designed to promote continuing education and improved competence of certified public accountants. We need to put into place a long-term mechanism for developing leading talent and for establishing continuing education in accounting. Most important of all is to be innovative in the initiation of training mechanisms and the development of talent at senior levels.

ENHANCING TRAINING FOR LEADERSHIP AND RAISING TALENT BUILDING TO A NEW PHASE

Why do we need to place particular emphasis on the development of leadership in the implementation of our talent strategy? The first reason has to do with the severe scarcity of talent at high levels in our profession, which contributes to our specific structural inadequacies. Rather than the typical organization structure in the form of a pyramid—with a handful of the elite at the top—in our profession, we have a frustum-shaped model, the main body of which represents the rank and file of our certified public accountants and on top of which we have an army of leading talents in accounting.

The current gap between the developed world and us can be expressed in quality, rather than quantity. This is manifested most clearly by the lack of significant numbers of senior and highly experienced practitioners. If we gave the market free rein, and waited for a rise in the general standard, an army of leading accounting talents would undoubtedly arise in our profession, but this process would take a long time, in the course of which a lot of opportunities would have been lost and we would have to pay a very high price. Therefore, it is paramount that we take action to accelerate both the process of producing leading accounting talents who are capable of competing in the international market, and the improvement of the general competitiveness of our certified public accountants.

The emphasis on leadership will act as a very effective catalyst for the improvement of the general quality of all of our practitioners. It will create a ripple effect, demonstrating that improvement can be made, and serving as a guiding role model for the whole profession. It will also help us focus on the review of our resources, consolidate our experience and reinforce our training efforts. We can also apply such experience to our work in further education in the mainstream, thereby killing two birds with one stone. The leading practitioners who emerge from our training will become role models. Their influence will help to motivate others in a continuing cycle of quality improvements for our profession. It is for these reasons that leadership development is such a key component in our talent strategy—a strategy within a strategy.

What kind of champions of accountancy do we want to produce? In other words, what kind of standards do we have in the development of talent? The answer to these questions can be distilled into one sentence: Equipping our talent with the knowledge and the capability they need, and helping them uphold integrity and professional ethics. Not only do they need to be knowledgeable, they must also be capable managers and leaders. Not only must they be skilful, they must also live up to the highest standards of integrity and professional ethics.

No one can become a leading figure in our profession without fulfilling these prerequisites.

Confucius, the most influential philosopher and educator in our history, placed strong emphasis on the importance of integrity and ranked it as a top priority in the development of talent. In the *Analects*, he argued that young people should "honor their parents while at home, respect their teachers and seniors while away from home, act with prudence and be trustworthy, be compassionate and extend friendship to the good, and apply themselves to the acquisition of fine art while they can." Obviously, what Confucius had in mind is shrouded heavily in the traditional Chinese philosophy of filial duty, respect for one's mentors, prudence, trustworthiness and compassion. What we have in mind nowadays has a stronger emphasis on the codes of professional ethics in socialism. The integrity we talk about here embraces not only such fundamental general principles as sincerity, trustworthiness, fairness and justice, which apply to all professions and industries, but it also covers the moral principles which apply in the CPA profession, such as maintaining independence to prevent any conflicts of interest in the instructions we receive. Such requirements are embodied in the laws and regulations governing the profession of certified accountants of all countries. There will be substantive developments and changes in the code of professional ethics in response to the development of the market economy and the CPA profession.

For instance, not long ago the Public Company Accounting Oversight Board (PCAOB) promulgated a new code of professional ethics for certified public accountants under the Sarbanes-Oxley Act in the United States to tighten the requirement for accountants to uphold independence as a key component in their code of professional ethics. This is also evidence of the need for professional standards to be updated and be more comprehensive in response to the forthcoming changes. Our champions of accountancy will be the trailblazers and role models in this.

Integrity can only be embodied in action and the observance of professional ethics only in real-life practices. Our profession needs to evolve along with the progress of our society. Certified public accountants form a community of professionals who serve their clients with their brains. Without a package of robust professional skills, no one is capable of taking on a professional leadership role.

That is why, in general, the standards for leading talents in accounting are centered on an inner quality, supported by an outward professional image, where knowledge, capability, integrity and high professional ethics are all key components. The specific requirements are as follows:

> *The establishment and entrenchment of a code of professional ethics which honors those who are sincere, honest and trustworthy and shames those who corrupt others or are themselves corrupt.*

Hu Jintao, our general secretary, has recently demanded the adoption of the socialist moral norms of honor and disgrace illustrated by the "Eight Dos and Eight Don'ts." This is a distillation and re-interpretation of our traditional Chinese outlook on duties, rights and virtues. It lays down our duties as members of society, as well as how we are expected to conduct ourselves as individuals. It embodies Chinese civilization and reflects our espousal of world civilizations.

Honesty and trustworthiness are two essential moral norms of a civilized society. It has never been more important to endorse these attributes and suppress greed than it is in today's society. Not only are they the crucial yardsticks in measuring how civilized we are and how highly we uphold our moral standards, they are also essential in telling others what our values are and where our society is heading. They are the fundamental principles of good governance and the backbone of a harmonious socialist society. An economy will only progress healthily and steadily when there is honesty and trustworthiness, upon which an orderly capital market and a creditworthy economic state are built.

As an important regulatory force in society, the certified public accounting profession abides by a code of professional ethics, with honesty and trustworthiness lying at its core. In an article entitled "The Profession of Chinese Accountants," published in 1933, Pan Xulun expounded on the significance and social values of honesty and integrity. He wrote:

> The *raison d'être* of the accountancy profession lies in the protection of the trustworthiness of commercial and industrial entities. Should it lose its own trustworthiness because of immoral acts, there would no longer be any reason for it to exist, thereby letting down the state and the people. We must therefore watch each step of our way.[2]

Essentially, certified public accountants are the standard bearers of the socialist moral norms with respect to honor and shame, and are required to act honestly and resist any temptation to engage in acts which bring shame on the profession. This is, on the one hand, a reasonable expectation of the profession in a socialist market economy, and on the other, a prerequisite for the healthy development of the profession. For champions in the profession, there is even more reason to abide by the principles of honesty and trustworthiness, to exercise correct judgment and to know what is honorable and what is shameful. Only in this way will we be able to serve others, build our career and devote ourselves to our country with honesty. Only in this way will our profession grow and prosper.

As we all know, the overall well-being of a society can be enhanced through the pursuit of personal gain by each individual in the operation of a market—a classic theory of the "invisible hand" espoused by Adam Smith. The right of individuals to pursue happiness and their own aspirations to realize their personal values should be recognized and respected, as long as they are allowed in a market economy. Meanwhile, however, as the protectors of a fair market, certified public accountants, especially those in leadership roles, should align their personal values with the development of the profession. In other words, it is incumbent upon them to have a strong sense of mission for our profession and of responsibility for society. They should harbor a strong desire to move the profession forward and see it as their duty to uphold fairness in the market and justice in society. When there are conflicts of interest between their personal gains as certified public accountants and social justice, market fairness and the overall well-being of the profession, they must not hesitate to make both material and spiritual sacrifices for the greater good of the wider community.

We must also recognize, in the meantime, that the strengthening of our sense of mission helps to provide a much firmer foundation for the realization of personal goals. By giving up improper short-term gains, we will ensure the long-term health and smooth development of both personal careers and corporate accounting practices. By integrating personal development into the growth of the profession, we will bring about a greater sense of satisfaction and create a higher social value.

Like all the other micro-members of the market economy, we face a lot of pressure from market competition. Nevertheless, I do not agree that profit maximization should be our profession's goal. Certified public accountants should shoulder even more social responsibilities and moral obligations than other professional practitioners. Highly-talented accountants should appreciate the fact that being recognized as such is an honor in itself. To leading talents in accounting, the true realization of personal values lies only in the integration of personal achievement and the growth of the profession, and in the public accolades they receive in the course of their work. They will be more target-oriented, direction-driven, confident and proud of themselves when they agree to take on more responsibility as the leading figures in the profession.

It goes without saying that professional competence is an indispensable component of the professional ethics of certified public accountants. I believe you all have the ability to improve in this respect. In addition to the ongoing accumulation of professional learning, you, as future leaders of the profession, will also need to focus on developing the following abilities and qualities:

First, it is necessary to develop **leadership and management ability**. You must learn to exercise influence and leadership over a project, a group or an accounting firm; and, on a larger scale, over a field or a profession. It is essential that top management is able to improve leadership, to accumulate and synthesize experience in the areas of policy-making, innovation, adaptation, command, planning, organization, coordination, human resources and motivation.

Second, you must have **strong communication skills** in order to build a harmonious profession. Ours is a very open profession, where communicating within the profession and with your customers is vital for developing business.

If we want other people to support us, we have to first ensure that they understand the points we are making. In this, effective communication is the key. As I see it, there are three major principles in communication: Timeliness (timely communication is also the least expensive); clarity (you must have a clear understanding of the specific purpose, content and expected outcome of the communication); and skill (the tone should be tactful, calm and objective in seeking understanding and support, rather than imposing your opinion on others). Mastering these basic essentials will enable you to achieve amazing results.

During the course of office communication with outside parties, you must learn to use your intelligence and be bold in seeking common understanding and a higher level of harmony. This kind of communication is based on sincere interaction rather than superficial politeness.

Third, it is necessary to build what I call **"partnership awareness,"** which is built around the spirit of cooperation. This spirit should permeate the structure of the organization, the way it conducts its business and the thinking of the staff as they work towards a common goal.

You must always be aware of the big picture, where every component of the office is viewed as a partner. You must abandon selfish departmentalism and work towards the development of the office as a whole.

All partners must be aware of their individual and collective responsibilities. You cannot have the attitude that a matter is of no concern to you and you will not get involved. You must be persistent in your approach when it comes down to any decision on matters that may harm the development of the office. You must have a strong sense of responsibility and a business mind to lead the office through ongoing, healthy development.

Fourth, we must **be tolerant**. Even our own fingers are of different sizes. Even brothers have conflicts. It is normal for partners to have different opinions and personalities. For issues and conflicts that do not involve matters of principle, you must be tolerant and be able to put yourself in the shoes of others. You must learn to improve understanding and resolve conflicts through positive communication.

In all things, we must **be fair**. Partners do not have special privileges. They must treat staff with fairness and respect. They must care about their staff and pay attention to their development to ensure that staff are united in their efforts to achieve the desired results.

The opening up of the Chinese economy and, with it, the internationalization of the accountancy profession, presents our profession with huge challenges and important opportunities. I hope you will all seize this rare historic opportunity to expand the worldwide development of the accounting profession and absorb the advanced ideas and experiences of other countries. In the meantime, continue to raise your own international accomplishments. Arm yourself with international thinking, international strategies and the spirit of international exploration. Aim to become the champion of accountancy who will one day be able to sign and issue audit reports for worldwide enterprises on the New York, London, Tokyo and Hong Kong Stock Exchanges.

Be Diligent, Good at Learning and Continue to Raise Your Level

To prepare for this time, first you must sharpen your tools. To become an expert in your field whose ideas are respected, first you must study diligently and grasp the concept of lifelong learning. It is even more important to adopt a scientific approach to learning. For me, learning focuses on and revolves around the word "awakening" as a means to achieving personal growth. Awakening through education and study opens the mind and enhances the ability to face and resolve new challenges.

At a training course of leading accounting talent in Shanghai last year, I outlined the basic requirements for those who wish to establish themselves as leaders within our profession, as follows: You have to be able to "understand yourself, learn from other people and prepare for the future; consolidate professional knowledge, form the network for knowledge, effect radical change, and promote." You must work hard to move in this direction.

Establish Life-Long Learning Awareness

The Sixteenth Party Congress promulgated the establishment of "a learning society where there is learning for all and learning throughout your whole life" to promote the comprehensive development of people and society.

In the 1960s, the French were the first to put forward the concept of lifelong education. The idea of a learning society was developed by the Americans. In today's knowledge economy, built around highly developed information technology, the knowledge and skills that served us in the past can no longer satisfy current needs for work and learning. The pressures of global development and competition make lifelong learning an essential requirement for all.

"Knowledge is power": We are all familiar with Francis Bacon's famous phrase which has encouraged so many successful people. Knowledge can change your fate and create your future. Your competitiveness depends on your strength which comes from your learning ability. Only people with high learning ability can compete with others and be successful. For highly qualified certified public accountants whose jobs rely on knowledge and intelligence, learning is even more essential. This kind of learning must not be looked on as an obligation imposed on you. Active learning should be part of your being. You must continue to add and learn new knowledge and skills; to improve your professional capabilities and management abilities; and to raise your competitiveness in the market.

Accumulate and Integrate Knowledge in Related Fields

To master a skill one needs to begin with something easy to grasp, and relevant knowledge and technology in related fields are good reference materials. Leadership requires a sound grasp of the specific knowledge and skills of your profession. But it also demands a more comprehensive understanding of related fields, such as the country's political and economic structure, its law, its history and the status and the function of intermediary organizations in the market economy. Being armed with such information will enable you to understand, consolidate and use your professional knowledge more comprehensively.

The training of top talent focuses on the integration of professional knowledge. You must be able to pull together all resources and make them work for you. You must be able to integrate many knowledge points to arrive at a correct professional judgment. You must form a network of related knowledge for mutual support, to bring change and improvement.

Diligence + Correct approach + Efficiency = Success

This was Einstein's famous formula for success, the most important factor being diligence. To develop the spirit of diligence, you must first strengthen your sense of responsibility towards society, establish the appropriate outlook on life, clearly define the purpose of learning and be determined to be successful. In a competitive market system, the superior will win and the inferior will be eliminated. If you are not diligent in learning, you will not be able to adapt to the requirements of the new society.

But you cannot be diligent for just a day or two; you must be persistent. A hard-working student who may not be very bright can still achieve better results and obtain greater success than a more intelligent student who is not prepared to put in the hard work required for success. Successful people possess a diligent spirit.

Embodied within the spirit of diligence is an approach in which you must learn hard, memorize well and think constantly. As Confucius pointed out, "Learning without thinking will lead to disappointment; thinking without learning is dangerous." To improve your knowledge and ability, you must study seriously and think thoroughly. You cannot do one and neglect the other. That is, "learn by studying classics and acquire profound knowledge through thinking."[3]

I personally have a habit of making brief notes of my perceptions and understanding of a certain issue. These are, of course, the result of thinking, and enable me to make observations and draw conclusions. They may only be a few words, but they sum up my point of view. Obviously, everyone has their own approach on how to learn, think and form conclusions, but these conclusions should not be merely a copy of what has been said before by others. It is more important to summarize your own perceptions and understanding.

Of course, your understanding will be broader and more well founded if it is the result of discussion with other people, who may have different perspectives on the topic at hand and may have come to a different conclusion on the matter. These conclusions may all be "correct." For example, experimenting with light can lead to two quite different conclusions: One that proves that light is a particle (a photon); the other proves that light is a wave. They are both characteristics of light. The conclusion we draw depends upon the viewpoint we have selected. If there were no communication between those who carried out the two experiments, they would always believe their respective conclusions to be correct because of the lack of counterproof. This applies too to the many propositions in the fields of social science. Having drawn our initial ideas through thinking, we should then test these by listening more to the opinions and suggestions of others. Only through communication can there be impact to produce the sparks in order to raise a higher standard. It is up to us to build the necessary platforms and bridges for communication and exchange, both in China and overseas.

In our country today, we have an environment that encourages innovation in society. Innovation is the evolution and development of knowledge. Innovative thinking is important in bringing about radical changes in knowledge. Einstein once said that we could not use the same approach to solving a problem that produced the problem in the first place. Innovative thinking and approaches are often necessary to solve problems.

Of course, to be innovative you must have a thorough understanding of the problem in the first place. You must have a sound grasp of the issues involved, and analyze them from different angles, weighing up the pros and cons to arrive at your conclusions.

Clearly, a few training courses alone cannot produce champions of accountancy. It takes time and a lot of effort to train talented individuals. We use the training to provide a system, a platform, an environment and opportunities for people with potential, and to promote and accelerate their growth. The training cannot rely on the efforts of the Ministry of Finance and CICPA alone. It needs input from many other directions in order to achieve the desired results. As I see it, there are four major requirements for the training of leaders in the CPA profession:

- Establish overall planning and system

  The training of leading talent is long-term project that will have a far-reaching effect on the profession as a whole. If it is to succeed, it will require a sound, scientific approach in drawing up practical plans and projects. The CICPA has drawn up a 10-year plan, based on the projected growth pattern in the accountancy profession, for the selection and development of leading talent through training with a multi-channel focus. While the plan is still being refined, it is envisaged that follow-up development for reserved personnel will be based on a three-year cycle divided into three stages: Selection, education and employment of talent. In the meantime, the system of examination and encouragement and the system of elimination are under further consideration. Only those with the potential and desire to undertake the huge responsibility that comes with being future leaders in the profession will progress to the next stage of the development project.

- Clearly define responsibilities and duties

  The training of leading talent is the concern of the entire profession and all must cooperate in assisting the CICPA in selecting the most suitable candidates from within the profession.

  The National Accounting Institute has pledged its full cooperation in the project and will work together with the CICPA to set up reasonable courses, assure the quality of teaching and focus on the effectiveness of development. The old saying, *"Give a man a fish and you feed him for a day. Teach a man to fish and you feed him for a lifetime*" is very pertinent in this regard. Instead of simply teaching people the information required, it is better to show them how to obtain such knowledge for themselves.

Offices of the Institute and CPA firms in various districts must raise awareness and support the selection and training of staff to create the necessary conditions for developing a pool of leading talents.

- Create opportunities through promotion

  To enable more certified public accountants to become part of the leading force mentioned earlier, we must step up the level of advertising to make champions of accountancy more well-known within the profession itself and in society at large.

- Establish goals and raise them gradually

  In order to achieve our overall goals, each member of the profession must have a practical plan for building a pyramid of success. Each must ask: Where do I want to be in my career 10 years from now, and what do I have to do to realize that long-term goal? What can I do in the next five years by way of a mid-term goal? What can I establish this year as a short-term measure towards achieving my long-term goal? What must I do every day, every week and every month in order to realize my short-term goal?

Any member who is determined to be successful can make good use of this approach. Great success is the accumulation of many small successes. When you keep on climbing the ladder towards success, the realization of your ideal becomes a matter of course.

The building of leading talents of the CPA profession is an important and enormous task. You are all outstanding professionals selected from among 700 people who sat the examination. You represent the best among the 70,000 certified public accountants. I hope you all value this opportunity. You must avoid being arrogant and being rash. You must be dedicated in handling the relationship between study and work appropriately. Maintain your youthful spirit, vitality and positive mindset for reaching higher. Remember your mission and do not let us down in this important task. I hope you will soon be able to apply your leading talent in this industry and make your own contribution to the internationalization of the CICPA.

ENDNOTES

1 Edited version of a speech given at the Inaugural Ceremony of the CPA Leadership Training Session, May 20, 2006.
2 In *Lixin Accounting Quarterly*.
3 The words of Yang Xiong (53 BCE–18 CE), a scholar and philosopher of the Han Dynasty.

Chapter 5

Innovative Thinking and the Pursuit of Excellence[1]

Anybody going through a period of change will experience a host of new challenges. But how does one effect the transformation from operative to manager? The key is to expand one's horizons. What I mean by this is to see more, hear more, reflect more and think more. By going through this process, reasoning becomes clearer, objectives more definite and methods more effective. Today, having four types of leading talents gathered to receive training together and to exchange opinions will undoubtedly help you to expand your horizons.

We all know that a good operative does what is asked of him by his superiors and no more, and that his level of responsibility cannot be compared to that of a manager. Some might say: "As an accountant, it doesn't matter how high you climb, you will still be checking the accounts." Others might say: "All you need to do is make sure that the books make sense; that is all there is for accountants." There is a certain logic to these arguments. Speaking as an accountant, I think that for an operative to learn and integrate a little more profession expertise is no bad thing because it enables him to apply the policies of his superiors more proficiently and flexibly. However, for this audience today and for leading talents in general, the job requirements are different because you have a different level of responsibility.

The manager of the financial and accounting system in a large corporation may be in charge of the financial department, but may also be in charge of its capital funding or be responsible for a particular project. Managers act as both bridge and bond between the corporation's operatives and its executives. Management accountants, general accountants, cashiers and auditors are all operatives whose job it is to carry out the orders of their superiors. What we need at this stage in the development of our profession are independent foot-soldiers, each of whom must be able to fight capably, and continually improve upon their ability to complete their duties independently. They must be familiar with business processes, proficient with business knowledge and focused on improving the quality and efficiency of their work.

However, meeting these requirements alone is not sufficient: Managers must also be able to lead, assist and promote others in such a way that self-improvement becomes collective improvement. Once an individual attains management level, he has to ally resourcefulness and intellect to his practical work, and he must have the ability to lead a team.

Thomas Edison's famous declaration that "Genius is one percent inspiration and 99 percent perspiration" gives due recognition to the place of hard work in any endeavor. As sculptor Wu Weishan sculpted the image of Master Hong Yi, spurred on by passion even as a storm raged around him, seized the inspiration and turned it into a masterpiece of sculpture. Inspiration is a splendid thing, but it can disappear just as quickly as it came. How can we create inspiration and how can we take advantage of it? Wu Weishan said that he created his masterpiece in a matter of a few days, but that he had been preparing the structural outline for nearly 10 years. That is why I believe that inspiration and accumulation are complementary and that neither thrives alone.

Many among you will have to undergo this transformation from operative to manager. As managers, we have to look at problems from a different perspective, which will enable us to make vastly different discoveries and benefits. Part of your role as managers will be to provide advice and suggestions to leaders or policymakers. It is important therefore that your suggestions are both scientific and reasonable. To be capable of giving this kind of advice you will need to open up your minds to new ways of doing things. As a manager you must learn to work within certain limitations or constraints and it would be a great mistake to assume that your every word will be accepted and acted on. We have to be flexible enough to find solutions.

When handling a situation, you will have to be flexible enough to know when to move forward and when to step back a little, taking into consideration who is charged with carrying out the particular matter and the extent of their responsibility. How and when will the work be done? Are there better ways of doing things? If things become difficult, what steps can be taken to redress the problems? We have to open our minds to different ways of doing things. But how do we open our minds? I have the following suggestions:

Firstly, we must fully utilize modern information technology to expand our minds. The American writer Thomas Friedman in his book *The World is Flat* has shown how internet technology has transformed our world, making it possible for anyone to access all kinds of information almost instantaneously. In doing so, it has leveled the playing field by taking knowledge (and, thus, power) out of the hands of the few and making it much more readily available to the masses. We can all make use of this capability to overcome the limitations imposed by our previous mindset, to open ourselves to new ideas and new ways of thinking.

Secondly, we can involve ourselves to a much greater extent in exchange and interaction with colleagues from other professions and fields of expertise. A former director of the American Federal Aviation Administration once said, "Never let people of the same profession eat at the same dining table." The unspoken implication here is that the nature of exchange and discussion between colleagues of the same profession is generally limited to that sphere of knowledge. The Japanese put it more bluntly by saying: "Integration is creation." People who study accounting and work in finance must communicate more and exchange ideas with people in other professions. Some people are suspicious that such exchanges may lead to their hard-earned ideas being taken over by others. My response to this is that, in most cases, this will not happen; and even if it does, it does not really matter all that much because the act of giving a rose leaves a sweet fragrance in your hand, which in itself is a meaningful event. Sometimes communicating and mixing with colleagues from other professions can bring enlightenment and open up a new vision, greatly enriching, modifying and completing your own way of thinking.

Thirdly, learn to use both sides of the brain, combining the logical with the creative. We are all accountants and, because the nature of the discipline, our left brains are more developed than our right. We find it easy to spend long hours considering minute problems and focusing on details and accuracy. However, in doing so we may not always be aware of the bigger picture, the larger ideas, concepts, directions and principles that make up the grander scheme of things. The specific nature of accountancy places emphasis on logic, on small details, and on calculations; it stresses the need for detail and does not generally encourage thinking outside the box or divergent thinking. This emphasis on logic is not always compatible with innovation and that is why as accountants we often display a tendency towards dispassionate rigidity. I would like us all to be able to break out of our professional frameworks and set our vision on greater concepts, while making use of the left brain to make detailed calculations. In this way, better, more definitive, plans can be made. We definitely need to break through the limitations acquired through 10-plus years of study and professional experience and try new ways of thinking, new angles for studying problems and analyzing issues. Specifically, we need to make the following three changes:

First, we should reverse our usual approach of looking at the small before moving on to the big. In our working lives, for example, we are used to considering operational management and corporate efficiency first before considering the bigger picture of profession in general and the development of the economy. As senior employees, you will need to see the bigger picture first in order to carry out your duties to a high standard within the scope of the company itself and within the profession at large. It is necessary to see the accountant's role from the perspective of the company's leadership and consider your actions in this light. It is only when you see your role in relation to the bigger picture that you will be able to position yourself correctly in relation to others.

Second, we need to move away from the tendency towards dismissing differences to valuing differences. As accountants, our strength lies in being able to notice differences and discrepancies when auditing accounts and analyzing reports. However, we are not particularly good at noticing differences when it comes to relationships with others or when making suggestions. This limits our abilities. The same sentence may make one person laugh but anger another. Saying different things to one person or saying the same thing to different people can have vastly different results. It is important to pay attention to the differences and afford them special consideration and focus.

Third, we need to become multidirectional in our thinking. You may have noticed that although many streets in our city are being repaired and widened, this still has not resolved the issue of traffic jams. This may be the result of one-directional thinking. If we design and repair the roads to just keep circling a point, a line or a ring, there may never be a resolution to the traffic problems. All situations are interconnected and exert some influence on each other. We need to become adept at listening to others, observing external factors and creating connections to enable our minds to think on multiple levels and from multiple perspectives.

FROM MANAGER TO LEADER

Leadership activities have been catalogued since ancient times. China's extensive archive of historical records from *Zuo Zhuan*, *Guo Yu*, *Stratagems of the Warring States* to *Records of the Grand Historian*, *History of Western Han* and then later to *History of the Three Kingdoms*, *The Political Program in Zhenguan Times* and *Comprehensive Mirror to Aid in Government*, and so on, all serve to a certain extent level as self-help textbooks for leadership. However, using experience to form a scientific explanation for the craft of leadership has only come about in the past two or three hundred years.

How does one determine the positioning of accounting managers and leaders? Within the financial and accounting system in a large corporation, for example, the head of the finance department is a leader. There are finance managers and accounting managers at the lower level and at the upper level there are chief accountants, financial directors and the CEO. The head of finance is at a mid-to-senior management level of the corporation's hierarchy and is responsible for important aspects of financial and accounting tasks under the directives of policy-making leadership. Strictly speaking, leaders are also categorized as managers, but managers are not necessarily leaders. So, where do managers and leaders differ specifically?

Former US President Richard Nixon made a highly philosophical observation when he said that managers do things right, while leaders do the right things. A manager thinks of today and tomorrow; a leader must think about the day after tomorrow. A manager represents a process; a leader represents a direction of history. A manager is nothing without a team to manage, but a leader retains a following even after leaving his post. This summary of Nixon's speech is probably more aimed at politicians but it applies equally well within the context of economics and accountancy. Professor Warren Bennis of the University of California believes that the manager focuses on systems and organization, the leader focuses on people; the manager maintains, the leader develops; the manager relies on control, the leader inspires trust; the manager has a short-range view, the leader has an innovative perspective; the manager asks how, the leader asks what and why; the manager has his or her eye always on the bottom line, the leader has his or her eye on the horizon. Other scholars suggest that while managers concentrate on situations and use people as tools, leaders concentrate on people and how to help them to fully and freely develop themselves. Managers often think of interests, objectives, tasks and work; leaders guide people to pay attention to values, visions, missions and significance. Managers often ask: What are our objectives and tasks? Leaders often state: These are our convictions, visions and missions.

Of course, all of this is open to discussion and a matter of interpretation and perception. However, our task is to determine how to become a competent leader, a leader who is deeply respected and trusted by all. The Chinese word for "leader" is derived from characters meaning "to guide the way" and "to supervise or oversee." A guide will pave the way ahead whereas a supervisor may sometimes be at the front, in the middle, but in most cases is standing at the rear.

This gives you some indication of the range of tasks with which you will be faced when you have attained the leadership level. You will need to consider the work of systems rather than just selected tasks. Your workload in relation to communication, negotiation and smoothing relationships will greatly increase compared to the simple untangling of small issues. You will need to conserve your energy to think about future situations and developments and not be bound by the present tasks at hand. You may not be able to fully estimate the practical details of every situation but you must promote advances in the important tasks and have a good grasp of their development. Because your status, your professional role, your seniority, your perspective, your management strength and reach, and your thinking will all change, so too must your methods. When faced with a collection of people with differing dispositions and characteristics, unevenly matched qualities and spanning all ages, and when faced with numerous areas to contemplate and all sorts of aspects of work to consider, a leader must have a comprehensive and accurate overview of the situation. How can this be done? I believe there are two criteria: regulation and supervision.

Some people believe that the primary purpose of a leader is to be a role model. To a certain extent this is true; hence the phrase "lead by example." However, for mid- to senior-level leaders, being a role model is not the most important thing. Rather, their primary consideration should be to set regulations and, in particular, to emphasize the use of these regulations. Good regulations can make good people of bad people; bad regulations can make bad people of good people. Time and history have provided countless examples of the truth of this.

Given that we must lead from the front and be good role models, it is even more important to focus on how to formulate regulations and strengthen leadership. Once others recognize your qualities and status as a good leader, you must gradually transform your leadership into supervision, making use of regulations to carry out inspections, promoting the implementation of all areas of work and inspiring a larger group of people to execute a greater amount of work. In order to be a real leader you must lead in ideas, coach in business, supervise on regulations and teach on conduct.

Whether formulating regulations or implementing supervision, we all need to learn how to express our thoughts, points of view and suggestions properly. We must never compromise on matters of principle and must be firm but courteous in expressing our views, being careful never to hurt the feelings of others as we do so. We must also have the grace to accept blame when we are wrong.

There is no easy way to become a good leader; it can only happen with concerted effort. Many experts here and abroad have studied this issue. In relation to the specific nature and actual circumstances of the accountancy profession, I want to stress the following points:

Develop dialectic thinking skills. Dialectic methodology is a framework for development in which contradiction plays the central role as the source of development and it is the essence of Marxist philosophy. Everything is made out of opposing forces or opposing sides, that is, contradictions. Leaders should apply dialectic thinking in their work so as to see the whole picture of things.

In this light, our leadership activities must emphasize the dialectic union of science and art, of standardization and motivation, of dichotomy and combination, and of complementary and opposing factors. In fact, in organizational leadership, this means always having in mind the dialectic relationship between issues such as primary and secondary, rigid and flexible, virtual and real, coarse and fine, strict and lenient, direct and indirect, general and specific, active and inactive, and so on. It is difficult to become a leader of superior quality without using dialectic thinking to maintain a balance in thinking, treating issues and handling circumstances.

Develop strategic thinking skills. Thoughtless strategy is blind strategy. Thought without strategy is superficial thought. At the core of strategic thinking is the notion of thinking for the complete entity. This is a basic quality and skill that all leaders must have. As a strategist, Zhugë Liang closely analyzed the overall situation in the country by comparing the strength of all the powers and their development trends. His solution for reuniting the divided three kingdoms is a prime example of strategic thinking that will be praised forever.[2] In order to rise to the rank of head of a finance department, accounting professionals must improve their strategic thinking ability, and place financial and accounting management and capital operations within the context of economic globalization and rapid advances in information technology. The changes in people's viewpoints, values and modes of behavior in the development of profession must also be placed within the practical realm of a socialist market economy.

Develop policy-backing skills. As advisors to corporate policy-makers or as important contributors to policy-making, the quality of the suggestions we make on such things as strategic investment, strategic actions, re-organization, financing and acquisition, or the re-formulation of processes will have a direct influence on the company's overall profitability and future development. Having the ability to provide the necessary support for policies requires that everyone understands development trends within their profession and the company's position vis-à-vis these trends. It also requires a complete familiarity with the company's business processes and a clear understanding of its financial circumstances such that financial risk to the company is minimized. In short, it requires that you become a one-person "think-tank" and center of knowledge for significant corporate policies.

Develop the ability to analyze and judge. Scientific analysis and accurate judgment are prerequisites for policy-making. The continuous strengthening and rapid development of information technology since our nation's reform and opening has brought many foreign companies to China and has taken many Chinese companies overseas. These companies face increasingly complicated market, industry and competitive environments that offer both opportunity and risk. More and more companies are linked by their supply chains and financial networks, which comprise trustworthy and non-trustworthy players as well as reliable and unreliable information. These environments require that we are all able to maintain genuine information and to eliminate false information in order to manage risks and promote development in a timely manner.

Develop innovative skills. Innovation reflects a nation's progressive spirit and provides unrestricted momentum towards its prosperous development. China has a long tradition of successful innovation within the financial and accounting management sector. Such practices and measures as team cost calculation, internal banking, cost veto, responsible accounting and comprehensive budget management have greatly improved and strengthened business management and increased economic benefits. Administrative units, professional accountancy and the theoretical field of accounting have also had good experiences in this regard. In the coming period, everyone should take extra steps to combine and reflect on their respective experiences with a view to expanding innovation in areas such as financial management, human-resource management and performance-assessment systems, value management models, accounting information technology, quality control and internal administrative control mechanisms, research into accounting theory, and so on.

Develop skills for internal controls. The financial scandals of Enron, WorldCom, Yin Guang Xia and China Aviation Oil clearly demonstrate the necessity of strengthening corporate controls. Strengthening internal control is fast becoming the entry ticket to capital markets for corporations and forms the basis of public trust. The State Department's leaders place extreme importance on internal control systems and repeatedly stress that "comprehensive company administration requires building comprehensive internal controls."

With the cooperation of the State-owned Assets Commission and the Securities Regulatory Commission, the Ministry of Finance has been given the task of leading the push to speed up research into internal control directives that will provide Chinese companies with a set of cohesive, scientific and authoritative control standards. On July 15, 2006, the Ministry of Finance announced the establishment of the Corporate Internal Controls Standards Committee charged with the task of creating a series of control systems over the next three to five years to guard against risks and prevent fraud. These systems are to be framed around control and assessment standards that are both suited to the continued development of China's market economy and are consistent with international standard practices. We must all do our utmost to assist the principals of organizations to promote the development of internal control systems and apply our skills to bring internal controls into line with regulations, increasing operational efficiency, ensuring the quality of information, and protecting asset security.

Become competitive on an international scale. We live in a time of limitless horizons, great structures and an enormous opening up from previous restraints. Some say that the world is fast becoming a global village. In an age when a single network wire can link the five continents and four oceans, it is inevitable that corporations, business units, accounting firms, researchers and educational organizations become involved in international trade cooperation and competition. International mergers and acquisitions, equity participation, stock market listing, restructuring and alliances have involved an increasing number of Chinese companies in international financial markets and trade sectors. In the face of fierce international competition, it is crucial to map out a strategy for internationalization and to capture the opportunities it presents. This involves accurately identifying the legal, cultural, and exchange-rate risks and then making reasonable choices as to the appropriate time and method of entering the international market. My hope is that everyone here will do their best to ensure our success on the international stage.

Develop communication and coordination skills. Good communication and coordination is an important condition for exchanging information, enhancing understanding, seeking support, promoting work, responding to complex issues and handling unexpected situations. Everyone here must do their utmost to develop and nurture the necessary skills to strengthen communication, both within their own organizations and with those outside. Your task is to enhance understanding, create interaction, convey empathy, dilute conflict, resolve problems and realize mutual success.

Develop skills to handle information. Given the unstoppable spread of information, financial and non-financial, we need to know how to manage it effectively so that it is put to the best possible use. People who raise their capabilities in collecting, studying and using information will hear and see more clearly.

Develop lifelong study skills. As Xun Zi said in *On Learning*: "There is never an end to learning." If we do not want our minds to age, our thoughts to become rigid, and our abilities to weaken, we must not regard learning as something that is done once and for all. Rather, we should take up the concept of lifelong learning as the key to work, life and happiness. We must always strive to strengthen our studies, by not being satisfied and by constantly seeking new knowledge and new challenges. Peter Senge, who popularized the concept of the learning organization, said: "The only advantage that one can take in the fierce competition that will come in the future is to study more quickly than others. It is true for countries, societies and organizations alike, and it is also true for leaders." We would all do well to keep this in mind.

THE PURSUIT OF EXCELLENCE: FROM LEADER TO POLICYMAKER

The concept of "policy-making" has been evident in Chinese literature since before the Qin Dynasty. Ancient texts such as *Han Feizi*, *The Art of War*, *Stratagems of the Warring States*, *History of the Three Kingdoms* and *A Comprehensive Mirror for Aid in Government* bear witness to this. There is a classical saying, "Devise strategies without going outside the tent and win battles from a thousand miles." This, I believe, captures the nature and essence of policy-making.

Let me use a large organization again by way of illustration. Policymakers fall into two groups. The first is the officers, such as chief accountants and finance directors, who have the power, the capability and the courage to make decisions in the management of one or several aspects of work within a corporation. The second group is the controllers of the corporation, who set the overall policies governing the corporation.

In the "pyramid" of corporate personnel hierarchy, the policymakers sit at the top, and they need the disposition and authority to oversee the unit as a whole and also the prudence and self-discipline not to abuse that position through the inappropriate use of power. In the process of rising through the various levels of the managerial pyramid—from the most basic operative levels to the most senior levels, from positions of silent presence up to positions of high power—a future policymaker will experience hardship in which, to borrow the words of Mengzi, "his mind [will be] exercised with suffering, his sinews and bones with toil. His body exposed to hunger and subject to great poverty."

Rising through the hierarchical structure requires a great transformation. Each step is a great leap towards maturity. We are quick to observe and praise the daring and determination of the policymaker but often overlook the accumulated wisdom and experience that have propelled the person into that role. As I mentioned earlier, management, leadership and policy-making are mostly made within constraints, and there is no unconstrained opportunity to make rash decisions at will. It is important that policymakers act with science as a prerequisite, with democracy as the means, with law as the basis, with power as the boundary, with management as a foundation and with service as a pivot, if they are to avoid setting rash or irresponsible policies.

To become a policymaker, a leader must:

- **Be able to make correct assessments in light of current trends.** Only leaders who can grasp situations accurately can respond appropriately to the needs of the time. China's increasingly strong economy and diplomacy provide a vast platform for the accountancy profession and a broad stage on which to develop a career in accountancy. Policymakers in the financial and accounting field must give deep consideration to how best to go about making correct assessments of current trends, of how to deepen reform and accelerate development, expand into new areas and new territories.

- **See the overall situation.** From this comes the ability to control. For example, during the policy-making process in the famous Three Main Campaigns of the Liberation War, Comrade Mao Zedong demonstrated the benefits of being able to see the overall situation clearly. First he chose Northeast China as a strategic direction, because he knew that controlling Northeast China would create a strategic stronghold that affects the rest of the country. During the Liao Shen Campaign he chose to take Jingzhou first and block the enemy's retreat, which gave him the upper hand in the entire campaign. While this was going on, he also deployed the Huai Hai campaign and gained a victory in the central plains. Whilst still in the throes of the Huai Hai campaign he secretly mobilized the North eastern troops to join the Northern troops in the campaign for Beijing and Tianjin. These campaigns were links of the same chain, accomplished in the same movement. As champions of accountancy and future policymakers, you must have a vision of the big picture, an awareness of the overall situation, concentrating your energies on overall, strategic issues. You must learn how to seize momentous events and use them to benefit the entire situation. If you cannot plan for the whole situation, you cannot plan for a single part of it.

- **See even the tiniest details.** This stresses foresight. The famous "frog experiment" serves as a good example. At the end of the nineteenth century, researchers at Cornell University conducted an experiment in which a frog was placed into a pot of boiling water. The shocked frog immediately jumped straight out and landed safely. Later, they placed it in a pot of cold water, where it moved about naturally, and then slowly heated the pot. Although the frog could feel the change in the ambient temperature, it did not immediately jump out due to its inertia. Later, once the water became too hot for it to bear, the frog was unable to jump out.

  As in this story, changes in the social environment are gradual and are not easily detected. If policymakers do not have a sense of crisis and a penetrating vision, they may not have the instinct to notice environmental changes or potential risks and this can lead to lamentable consequences. For this reason, a good leader and policymaker must improve his ability to pick up on the tiniest clues, to nip problems in the bud, to consider and handle problems with a degree of foresight. He must be able to seize upon trends even when they are only sprouting, so that he can anticipate future developments and formulate policies ahead of the game.

- **Be broadminded.** It is my experience that the basic requirement for broadmindedness is the pursuit of the greater good at the expense of the individual good. All policies have consequences. For these consequences to withstand the tests of actual practice, history and the masses, self-interest must be overcome. The narrow interests of the individual, of the department or of the small collective must not be allowed to hold sway. At the same time, it is particularly important for leaders and policymakers to maintain clarity and to pool wisdom from a wide array of suggestions. In our profession, policy-making deals with such things as the cost of finance, return on investment, asset security and public interests. Only forward thinking, fair-minded people with integrity and an ability to handle the relationships between the individual and the collective, between short-term and long-term interests, and between corporate and public interests will make significant progress along their chosen career path.

- **Improve mental strength.** The process of policy-making is also a test of mental strength. Without a healthy, mature and stable approach, a single surprise or shock can cause a policymaker to waver. The sporting world has the Clark phenomenon, which is when superior athletes are unable to perform to their competitive level because they become overwhelmed by nerves. I hope that whilst fulfilling your duties you all make efforts to forge a positive, firm mindset that will react to change with equanimity. Only then will you be able to truly bear the heavy responsibility of a policymaker.

In making policies scientifically, there are numerous points to keep in mind.

First, you must take account of all aspects and strike a balance. In worldly affairs, particularly those at the policy-making level, perfection is unlikely ever to be found. Sometimes, if a policy or a plan attracts no major objections, and if everyone can benefit from it to a certain extent, then this may be the best that can be hoped for. Take, for example, Shanghai's Xin Tian Di district.[3] There, the elderly can visit and relive old times, while younger people can visit and feel very trendy. When Chinese people visit the area, they feel as if they are abroad, and when foreigners visit, they feel that they are in China. A meeting of different cultures can produce an even greater culture; a meeting of viewpoints can promote a blend of thoughts and can be applicable to the world at large. Things do not exist in isolation; they often involve several departments or systems and are restricted by all types of conditions, making it necessary to consider a whole range of factors and not oversimplify things. Perfection can be pursued as a personal decision, because it is a personal matter. But the choices made for society, or choices made for business objectives, or policy choices in accountancy can never be perfect. I am not saying this to relieve anyone of their responsibility to give their utmost to create a bright future, and it is not to encourage you to go about your days ignorantly or to think that "almost" is good enough. I say it to implore you all to consider situations fully, work together and strike a balance of interests among all related parties, and then make an accurate policy.

Next is the need to pay attention to the big picture and focus on motivation. This is an important point. The old saying "flames can reach higher if everyone gathers firewood" is very applicable here: Fully mobilizing the enthusiasm of every member of staff is a key element to becoming an excellent policymaker. As a high-level leader or a policymaker, you are responsible for igniting the energy and enthusiasm for work of your subordinates. If you order your staff to do things just because you are in a position to do so or if you hand out harsh punishment for minor offences and allow no room for opposing suggestions, then I do not believe you are a good leader.

"When water hits a rock it sounds, when a man is motivated it can turn into greatness."[4] Motivation in this case might mean giving people the leeway to solve problems for themselves; although, of course, you should help where help is needed. You can stretch the administrative distance between yourself and your colleagues but you must reduce the psychological distance between you. In this way you will make everyone willing to work with you and do their jobs well.

Thirdly, learn to prioritize and place importance on methods. Policy-making is hard because of choices; choices are hard to prioritize and prioritizing is hard to rationalize. How we rationalize our priorities and how we choose rational policies comes down to method. I have suggested to my daughter that before she finds a partner, she should make a list of her main criteria and prioritize them. From this she will know whether she should pursue a particular relationship and it might increase the chances of success and help her avoid a lot of pain that can come by doing things in the reverse order.

Colleagues: I have spoken of my knowledge, feelings and experiences about the transformation from an operative to a manager, from a manager to a leader and from a leader to a policymaker. You may or may not agree with all that I have said. What I want to stress is that in effecting these three big transformations, there is no sudden shift or overnight change. It is a long, slow and arduous process. Our society currently faces a time of great change and we ourselves are also in the state of transition. I hope that throughout this process we can all gain more knowledge, draw more from the teachings of others, integrate our own characteristics in our thoughts, be inspired, become more mature through thinking and inspiration, and spare ourselves unnecessary detours and hardships. Like you, I still have a long way to go, and together we shall accumulate knowledge little by little, through the 99 percent of perspiration and the 1 percent of inspiration.

As I told the CPA leadership training session, integrity must always come first. Chinese CPAs have to enter the international arena and build their brand and reputation. As I have said in other sessions, your work has to be more widely citable across disciplines other than accounting; your research and your students have to be more useful to society at large. I expect that, in the not-too-distant future, your presence in the financial and accounting teams in state-owned large- and medium-sized corporations, national institutions, business units, intermediary agencies and various industries will result in improvements in the management and competitiveness of Chinese corporations and China's economy. I expect to see you standing tall on the international economic stage; I expect to hear your voices at the podium of international academic conferences; I expect you to find commanding heights and the right to speak in all areas of the international accounting sector.

Remember, though, that successful leaders are not made by training alone. Leading talents have particular personalities which bloom as they learn and practice. Leadership is the result of an individual's sensitivity, intellect, potential and mindset crystallized at a certain time and under certain conditions. There is an old saying: "Literary works are valuable only when they are original, and heritage is genuine only when it is passed on." Each must grasp his/her own golden touch in order to make continuous progress.

As the old saying goes, the masters usher us through the gate, but a pious life depends on the individual. Tens of millions of accountants await your growth, your advancement and your future development; your colleagues, friends and family all place high hopes on you; the three National Accounting Institutes have great expectations of you; the Ministry of Finance, the Ministry of Personnel and the Chinese Institute of Certified Public Accountants and the Accounting Society of China have high hopes for you. I hope that you can bear great responsibility, that you can create fine work and that together you can create a splendid future for the Chinese accountancy profession and write a new chapter in its great development.

ENDNOTES

1 Edited version of the speech given at the National Senior Accountants Joint Training Session, September 20, 2006.

2 The famed third-century Chinese strategist Zhuge Liang was visited in his cottage by the warlord Liu Bei seeking a way to overcome the rival Wei and Wu states in the Three Kingdoms of Shu. Zhuge Liang drew up a long-term strategy (the Longzhong Plan) that enabled Liu Bei to defeat the other two and reunify the empire of the fallen Han Dynasty.

3 This is an historic area of the city. The traditional Shikumen tenement buildings have been preserved and the area has been redeveloped into a trendy café and entertainment district.

4 A quote from Qiu Jin (1875–1907), an anti-Qing Empire revolutionary, feminist and writer. She was executed after a failed uprising and today is considered a hero in China. This quote is used to stress the importance of motivation to help one grow and become a great person.

A Good Essay is the Result of Good Subject Matter; Steady Progress is the Result of Strong Resolve[1]

Colleagues: As we are accountants by profession, it is somewhat hard to avoid the stench of money rubbing off on us. However, Minister Ye Xiao Wen researches religious practice and, as I said this morning, "If you give someone a rose, your hands will retain the fragrance." His comments this afternoon regarding doctrinal teachings have lifted the scent and a sweet fragrance is wafting all around us.

It is from this "altar" that Minister Ye has suddenly transported us away from the click-clacking of our working abacus to the bells and music resonating inside a place of worship; away from our calculations of economic profit to the tide of compassionate thought in a sacred hall. He has enabled us to bathe in the sun, cleanse our spirits, open up our minds and explore the mysteries that lie between conflict and harmony.

In the face of the theory and ideology of extensive and profound knowledge:

Do you realize your own insignificance?

Do you realize the vastness of the world?

Do you realize how fascinating the world is because of its contrasts of opposition and unity, conflict and harmony?

Do you realize that accountancy and religion are related?

Do you realize that conflict is a prelude to harmony and that harmony is the result of conflict?

Do you know why there are so many people who are willing to sacrifice their lives or even their own wives and wailing children?

Maybe these things are all related to faith.

What is faith? Faith is devotion to an ideal. For the sake of this belief, people would sacrifice their own lives; and do so happily!

What is our ideal?

It is to reinvigorate the accounting profession in China, to globalize Chinese accounting practices and to create a harmonious and prosperous society.

Colleagues: Are you willing to abandon selfish desires and transient interests in pursuit of your ideals? Are you willing to strive relentlessly and contribute more for your ideals?

In the *Three Kingdoms*[2] it is written that: "In matters under heaven: That which has been long divided, will be united and that which has been long united, will be divided."

Religious teachings tell us that: "In matters under heaven: That which has long faced conflict, will be united and that which has been long united, will face conflict"; life starts with death.

We should bid farewell to our past identity as operatives or implementers and welcome our future identity as managers, leaders and policymakers. Let us all calmly resolve to strive for our ideals!

Colleagues: Minister Ye spoke of three types of harmony: harmony between man and nature; harmony amongst men; and harmony with oneself. The hardest to achieve is harmony with oneself. How can one be at harmony with oneself? From my understanding, it is mainly achieved by learning to be grateful.

Thanksgiving is not just a religious act but also an act of wisdom and morality. The English writer Thackeray wrote: "Life is a mirror. If you frown at it, it frowns back; if you smile, it returns the greeting." If you are grateful in your life, life will grant you brilliant sunshine. People driven by gratitude in their heart are different from others; they are solid and selfless, humanitarian and loving, kind, dedicated and devoted, full of responsibility and a sense of purpose.

If we could cherish our lives and be grateful, there would be more harmony between us and less estrangement; more unity and less friction. We would find more ways to resolve issues and complain less. If you applaud others, you will hear applause around you and if you help others, success will follow you; looking after others is to look after yourself.

Let us constantly improve our self-cultivation and achievements with a grateful heart, endlessly serve our community, give back to our people and shoulder our responsibilities. Let us be people who earn respect from others, of whom our families are proud and who merit great esteem in the accounting profession and other industries alike.

Master Xing Yun said: "Where there is Dharma, there is a way."

Zhao Pu-chu said: "There is a good essay where there is subject matter."

Minister Ye told us: "Progress starts with resolve."

I say to you all: Professional success will come when harmony prevails in your mind and in the external environment.

Let us give another round of heartfelt applause to thank Minister Ye for his brilliant speech!

ENDNOTES

1 A commentary on the speech by Minister Ye Xiao Wen at the Accountancy Leadership Training Program Conference (a reporting back session of joint training program for leading accounting talents), September 20, 2006.

2 *Romance of the Three Kingdoms*, written by Luo Guanzhong in the fourteenth century. A historical novel based upon events in the turbulent years near the end of the Han Dynasty and the Three Kingdoms era (169–280), it is regarded as one of the four great classical novels of Chinese literature.

Chapter 7

Studying Philosophy: Clear Directions at a Glance[1]

In the past two years, the training program of leading accounting talents has achieved outstanding results. There are currently 307 people from four talent categories and nine training batches, of whom eight have been appointed chief accountants, five professors and six PhD supervisors. Seven have become partners, five have been included in the Ministry of Education's "Program for Supporting Outstanding Talent of the Century," nine have been employed as consultants with the Ministry of Finance's Internal Control Standards Committee, and more than 200 people have published more than 400 articles, covering more than 200 State-level and ministry-level scientific research projects from various categories.

At the same time that our training work is receiving increasing recognition from the accountancy profession, it is also receiving greater approval from parties outside the profession. Our task of creating "one brand, one concept, one standard" is a very difficult one. I hope that the foundation of the "10-Year Plan for the Cultivation of National (Prospective) Leading Accounting Talents" by the Ministry of Finance will open the process further, so that the systematic, scientific training methods will provide better conditions for the maturing of our students. For this, we will need to develop innovative and effective systems.

Before this trip to Xiamen, I have been studying at the Party School of the CPC Central Committee; there the study of philosophy has been particularly enlightening for me. Even as I was taking a relaxed stroll through the gardens of philosophy, and bathing in the illuminated thoughts of philosophers from the past, I was reflecting on the past, present and future of accounting. Accounting needs philosophy, while philosophy stimulates and promotes the development of accounting. Here, I would like to share with you some insights on the relationship between accounting and philosophy.

THE AFFINITY BETWEEN ACCOUNTING AND PHILOSOPHY

What is the world? It is the movement of the material continuum, which has its own independent basis and performance; that is, its essence and phenomenon. Science makes use of its knowledge of "existing entities" to interpret natural phenomena and the internal connections that link them. Philosophy makes use of its knowledge of "existence" to explore the nature of the world and the internal basis for the phenomenal world.

What is the nature of the world? While Western philosophy and Chinese culture have different explanations, they both, surprisingly, use "numbers" to sum up their concept of the world. The ancient Greek philosopher Pythagoras said, "All things are numbers." Numbers are the basic building blocks of the real world, and numbers can be used to explain everything. The ancient Chinese philosopher Lao Tzu said, "The Dao produced one, one produced two, two produced three, three produced all things." All things on earth can be explained by using "numbers" such as "one" and "many." This is obvious. Using numbers to sum up the nature of the world makes it possible to integrate knowledge and praxis along the pathways of understanding what the *Book of Changes*[2] calls the "cycle of the beginning and the end." The knowledge and grasp of the "numbers" which are inseparable from the material forms would also stimulate and promote the understanding of the materialist interpretation of history. In this way, numbers can be used to understand, describe and change the world, and bring accounting and philosophy into a more intimate relationship.

The objectives of both subjects are consistent with each other. In the process of searching for truth, philosophy attempts to explore the general nature of things, eliminates the complex scenarios and the confusing, misleading illusions of the phenomenal world, and strives to develop a common and accurate understanding of objective matters. When accounting is used to measure and report the economic activities of accounting entities, it also strives for truthful computation and comprehensive feedback. In a certain sense, truth is the core nature of accounting; from this perspective, the research objectives of accounting and philosophy are consistent.

The research pathways for both subjects are related. Philosophy provides an understanding and summary of the world, while accounting is the control and conceptual summary of economic activities. The book-entry accounting principle that "every transaction consists of debits and credits and the value of the debits must be equal to the value of the credits" and the resulting debit–credit relationship is a manifestation of philosophical thought on the ordinary relationship between things. The debit–credit relationship is like the laws of cause and effect in the universe, and the correspondence between the use of funds and the source of funds that results from the double-entry accounting system is similar to the *yin* and *yang* discourse in traditional philosophy. The concept of the balancing of accounts also interprets at a certain level the principle of energy conservation in economic life; and the assumption of the going-concern in accounting has many similarities with the principle of sustainable development in philosophy. On this basis, too, it can be said that accounting is an academic discipline born out of, rooted in and developed from the philosophical realm.

The achievements of the research for both subjects are mutually interactive. Taking this a step further, the most fundamental and universal laws that are described in philosophy would inevitably guide the progress and development of accounting. Furthermore, accounting is an example of the philosophical system in the economic realm; its search to present a true representation of the state of economic activities is similar to the quest for truth in philosophy. The practical methodologies used in accounting for obtaining and processing information are similar to philosophy's investigation of all things and its striving to maximize knowledge. Accounting research on business language is similar to modern philosophy's extensive investigations of semantics. Therefore, we can boldly assume that a major breakthrough in accounting theory could make a contribution towards the development of philosophy.

Philosophical cultivation improves the essence of life in accounting. The study of philosophy confers many benefits, which can be classified into two broad categories: The elevation of the state of the mind; and the elevation of the cognitive abilities.

In relation to the first category, Feng Youlan[3] suggested that philosophy can "elevate the human soul to transcend the real world and experience values that are higher than morality." Dr. Fu Peirong, from the University of Taiwan, said, "If we depart from life, philosophy is empty; if we depart from philosophy, life is blind."

We live in a multifaceted, complex, materialistic world and the pursuit of materialism often leads to people becoming enslaved by external things without their being aware of it. Conversely, those who achieve a state of high philosophical cultivation are not trapped by the trivialities of life, and will not sink into simplistic materialistic pursuits. They are able to observe, reflect upon and analyze complex phenomena dispassionately, which allows them to respond to changes in the external world free from materialistic entanglements.

"Excellence" is another ideal state that is sought after in philosophy. It requires the building of a self-consciousness and personal autonomy in the lives and lifestyles of people to guide them to develop in the right direction in the search for true value.

When confronted with a complex web of contradictions, most people either become frustrated and restless or follow the crowd. Conversely, accountants who have a high attainment in philosophical cultivation should be able to consciously follow the rules of reason and ethics in assessing and choosing between right and wrong, honor and disgrace. They should be unwavering in their ideals and integrate these into their daily lives and their careers. Of course, the values manifested in their work and career would also receive more recognition and feedback from society.

WHY DO WE EMPHASIZE THE NEED TO STUDY PHILOSOPHY?

Hegel said that there are two paths in the study of philosophy: The ordinary path, across which people walk wearing casual clothes; and a path filled with people wearing the robes of the high priest, who have noble sentiments towards the eternal, the sacred and the infinite. Our discussion today encompasses three groups of people. The first is the general public, who do not aspire to "wearing high priest's robes" and are more receptive to philosophical wisdom that is clearly explained and easy to understand. The second encompasses what I refer to as the profession elite—a group of people of independent spirit, rich creativity and a passionate sense of responsibility to serve society. They are the core group that leads the healthy growth of the economy and society. Their job requirements and social mission have determined that they need to have a profound understanding of the basic principles of philosophy, from which they can self-consciously and freely make use of the philosophical principles and methods to advance and promote the healthy development of their work and career. The third encompasses learned scholars and philosophers. They possess a very high level of philosophical cultivation, have an understanding of the exceptional way and the pioneering spirit of trendsetters, and are able to pass on their wisdom and creativity, thereby raising the philosophical cultivation of the entire nation.

Clearly, our champions of accountancy belong to the "profession elite." They should take the lead in studying philosophical thought to enable them to stand at the forefront of the times, and advance the major reform, improvement and development of the accountancy profession.

Having analyzed the function that philosophical cultivation has in improving the essence of life in accounting, we will now analyze the important role of philosophical cultivation in improving our cognitive abilities.

Philosophy can help us to manage the big picture. Human experience is messy and scattered, which results in a fragmented vision. Nevertheless, some people strive to gain an overall understanding of life and have an overall grasp of the world and society, in order to make more effective choices. The importance of strategy can be seen here, and the importance of philosophy is also found here. By having a good grasp of philosophy (which is known as the "greater wisdom"), one is able to develop insight into the essential nature, trends and "big-picture" issues underlying multifaceted and complex things. Philosophy is not a simple theory, weapon or tool that can be used to solve concrete problems. However philosophy is able to help people to maximize their potential, and to prevent them from neglecting the big picture and committing errors caused by looking only at isolated incidents on which to base their conclusions.

Philosophy enables us to travel from the low plains of everyday thinking to the more rarefied atmosphere of the higher plateaus of thought. Though it may not be possible to dwell there for a long period of time, it allows for the vision to be broadened, providing an overview of all the surrounding roads and mountain ranges. From here it is possible to gain a comprehensive understanding and appraisal of the overall character and value of accounting and the accounting life.

The Xiamen National Accounting Institute has a very good geographical location—facing the sea and surrounded on three sides by mountains—to illustrate the point. If the sea represents the world, the mountains represent a kind of "Great Wall" made up of more than 12 million accountants encompassing your units, the Ministry of Finance and our mother nation. We want to build the mountain a little higher and make it more stable, provide everyone with a more solid foundation from which to take bigger strides towards the global community. To this end, we are vigorously implementing the three major developmental strategies: Aligning accounting with international standards; training elite accounting talent; and promoting the internationalization of accounting firms. We are also gradually launching other major strategies to set up the internal control system, to modernize accounting practice and expand research into accounting theories. After this we will begin preparations for the two major strategies of scientific management for the "accounting command post" and accounting feedback to society. Together, these eight major strategies are designed to provide overall services to all areas of accounting work, financial work, the economy and scientific development.

Philosophy can help us to strengthen our thinking. There is a Jewish saying: "When humanity thinks, God begins to smile." The thinking tools that we rely on for understanding the world are not comprehensive and perfect. But like other tools that we use in our daily lives—kitchen knife, gas, electricity and car—if we know how to use them, we will be able to function more efficiently and with less effort. If we don't know how to use them correctly, we will cause harm to others as well as to ourselves.

The significance of philosophy for thinking is as follows:

Philosophical thinking can help prevent people from falling into the common traps of human thinking. One of these traps is to take the view that things can suddenly come into existence and can be abruptly extinguished without any cause or reason and without any past or future. They do not see the interrelationship between things or phenomena but make a presumptuous judgment. Another common trap is to view issues as simply being mechanical and unchanging, and allow no possibility of advancement with the times. The thoughts of philosophy regarding universal connections and dialectical development are the best weapons to counter such tendencies. Friedrich Engels pointed out: "If a nation aspires to stand at the pinnacle of science in the world, theoretical thinking must not be absent even for a single moment." At the same time, he also said, "In order to enhance the capacity for rational thinking, apart from learning philosophy there is no other way." The study of philosophy allows one to maintain a dialectical perspective when interacting with people and things, to have a clear understanding of the truth and falsehood and the ins and outs of the various phenomena which confront us, and have the utmost control over their development. A life like this is a life of wisdom.

Language and logic: The major tools of human thinking. Men perceive the world through their senses, and all these feelings are converted into linguistic signals and processed through the brain. If language is the expression of the thinking process, logic is its driving force. Using these two items, people are able to formulate thoughts to understand the world. A philosophical methodology is able to organize the thoughts of men at the fundamental level and improve speaking and behavioral capabilities, derive systematic cognition from complex phenomena, clarify the mental roadmap for work, highlight the work priorities and specify the direction for hard work. Methods are tools and can be used for greater competitiveness. We can achieve good performance only when we have good tools; philosophical logic serves as the tool and method for thinking. The functions of logical analysis and conceptual summary can be applied to accounting at a high level, and enable a high degree of abstraction and generalization to be performed on complex accounting problems. Accountants must learn to summarize the lessons from their personal experiences and from those of other disciplines; they must integrate the wisdom from within their own profession with the combined wisdom of people from different industries and different countries; they must learn the techniques and tools for management and administration, and understand the different human values and dialectics.

Linguistic expression is an important component of the ability to think. Although we speak every day, there are times when we cannot find the words to express our ideas or emotions. The ability to give clear expression to our thoughts in words that others can understand is a very important quality to nurture. Everyone loves to hear the speeches of our comrade Li Ruihuan[4] because his speeches are illuminated with rational thoughts. He writes these speeches himself, which reveals his personal perspectives and experience. His words are stimulating and inspirational and take him beyond the concrete issues being discussed. They demonstrate a form of political wisdom and very high standards of philosophical thinking. He pays particular attention to the words he uses in examining both sides of an argument, and uses analogies and witty wordplay to explain the issues and illustrate his principles.

Comrade Li Ruihuan's thinking is philosophical and extremely profound. I would strongly recommend two of his books to everyone: *The Study and Application of Philosophy* and *Random Thoughts on Dialectical Materialism*. At the same time you should also look at commentaries on the books. Reading and understanding them may liberate us from shallow thinking.

Reaching biased conclusions and presumptuousness are two bad habits which philosophy can correct. Restricted by the limitations of epistemological tools and cognitive capabilities, human beings do not possess the ability to instantly understand everything. For example, we cannot instantly make a comprehensive and systematic assessment of the business status of an enterprise, and can only make a preliminary diagnosis of the financial matters. Man's understanding of the world is based on the extension of existing knowledge to deduce the whole based on the knowledge of the parts, and to deduce the infinite from the finite. This process is a bit like a blind man groping around; and if the information collected in this way is incomplete, it is easy to draw a biased conclusion. Where there is excessive self-confidence, it is easy to be presumptuous.

Philosophers believe that the acquisition of knowledge is a process that is continually growing deeper, and one of moving towards absolute truth. The relativity of human knowledge lays the theoretical foundation for reflection and critical analysis. My philosophy teacher said the following:

> China is currently developing into a full-fledged global super-power, and plays an increasingly important role in the international community. Therefore, in relation to our country, the growth of the economy and society may be important, but important aspects of philosophy such as the quality of ideological ethics and theoretical thinking ability are of equal importance. If we lack such ethical quality and theoretical thinking ability, it will be impossible for a developing country like China to naturally gain a foothold in the world and to truly play the role of a global superpower.

I wonder, isn't it the same for accounting as well? The accounting community in China is taking steps into the international arena, and is gradually expanding its influence in the international community. The importance of the accountancy profession is being increasingly and widely recognized, but currently what we lack most is the theoretical thinking ability in philosophy. This is also one of the root causes for the inadequate work that is done in the area of innovation in major accounting theories. The basic method used by Socrates involves rhetorical and dialectical discourse, and then summarizing that discourse to formulate universal concepts or definitions. The many concepts that we derive from accounting work are usually derived from habitual practices or immediate demands, to the extent that there is little opportunity to carry out critical reflection. How could there be any significant innovation or discovery? Rene Descartes, who saw the value in methods, used inquiry into doubt as a method, with the objective of finding a point of absolute certainty. His famous saying "I think, therefore I am" should become a guiding principle for all of us as accountants in our inquisitive and rational search for the truth.

Philosophy can help everyone to create new ideas. As a special method for understanding the self and the objective world, philosophy has transcendental characteristics. Because of its generality and universality, philosophy is able to refute available and existing things. Science solves problems, while philosophy creates problems. Philosophy promotes critical and innovative thinking in accounting, extending new ideas, consolidating new concepts and raising new problems. Without this, accounting would remain static, unable to see beyond its own very small circle, and thus unable to promote necessary improvement, reform and development. Therefore champions of accountancy must learn philosophy, achieve "broad learning, deep questioning, careful thinking, clear clarification and faithful action,"[5] and learn to examine, reflect on and criticize every aspect of economic activity and accounting work. Only in this way, can economic activity and the accounting profession develop along a rational path.

Concepts such as the normal distribution curve in statistics and the Gini coefficient in economics are very scientific, integrated academic subjects. Through a linear approach or a single concept, all the whys and wherefores can be understood, and a particular developmental phase or a particular economic phenomenon can be summed up. Why does accounting and finance not have such concepts? Financial concepts are all simple ratios; there are no integrated indices. A simple ratio can only provide answers to simple problems and summarize simple phenomena, but cannot carry out an integrated, systematic and generalized description of complex phenomena. After you have completed talking about a list of ratios, your boss or partner would have been frustrated by what they are hearing, or might not even be able to understand what they are hearing. Conversely, when we combine the Gini coefficient and the Kuznets inverted U-curve in economics, we will be able to clearly illustrate the degree of connection between the phases of economic development, the income distribution gap, and harmony and stability in society, and provide people with an infinite space for imagination. What accounting lacks is a similar step of major creation, major revolution and major progress. It lacks the capacity to innovate on the basis of criticism and to advance on the basis of denial. When accounting reflects the business activities of an enterprise, can it also use a graph to describe its developmental process, or to compare its development with that of other enterprises in the same industry or in other industries? Each discipline has its own unique regulatory concepts, which can have simple expressions but deep and profound meaning. Can accounting create more of such inventions that are rich in regulatory characteristics and easy to understand? I invite all of us to think about it and put in more hard work in this area.

Philosophy can help everyone to plan for the long term. Without a strong and visionary leader, it would be difficult for any industry, discipline, institution or organization to achieve success; accounting is no exception. Comrade Li Ruihuan described philosophy as "a mysterious discipline" and continued:

"The more your work changes and the newer it is, the more useful it seems to be; the higher your position is and the bigger the occasion, the greater are its effects; the more difficult and complex the problems you face, the more amazing are its results; the more critical the problems you confront, the more critical its effects become."

As he sees it, philosophy has a unique function in increasing the quality and abilities of leadership. In order to become a future champion of the accountancy profession and a respected and credible leader, you must equip yourself with, and learn to use, philosophical theories, methods and thinking to guide your work.

HOW TO MASTER PHILOSOPHY

A professor from the CPC Party School told me, "Do not assume that by having learnt philosophy today, you will be able to apply it tomorrow; do not expect that when you encounter concrete problems, you will be able to find the way to solve the problem merely by browsing through a textbook on philosophy." As He Lin puts it, "Philosophy is a type of academic cultivation, and is hard work where action is guided by the truth." Philosophy has a huge ideological system and systematic theories and methods. Following is a summary of the four basic areas that we need to grasp when we study philosophy:

Method to gain a deep understanding of philosophy: The methodology of philosophy deals with the theory of methods, and involves the refining and summarizing of methods, and may be viewed as the method of methods. Having a grasp of it is particularly helpful to us for handling various contradictions and problems. The key points of the methodology of philosophy are as follows:

First, understand the situation. In accordance with the principles of philosophy, understanding the situation requires us to start by defining the objectives and, giving due respect to objectivity, undertaking in-depth studies. Understanding the situation falls within the subject of "the investigation of things" in philosophy, and its core elements are comprehensiveness and objectivity. This requires us to understand both internal and external aspects of things, and to understand the past, present and future of things, and to search for the truth based on facts. Only in this way can we achieve multiple applications for a single case and obtain the maximum returns for our efforts.

Second, analyze the contradictions. Contradictions exist everywhere. The analysis of contradictions falls within the "extension of existing knowledge" phase. The root cause of the contradictions is determined by seeking out insights into their true nature. Contradictions come in many forms: big and small; primary and secondary; internal and external; and human and material. The analysis follows three major phases—positioning, sorting and summarizing—through which the contradictions are screened, classified, and arranged in order of priority to eliminate unnecessary details and extract the essence of each. The process clears the way for us to then take the bull by the horns, grasp the core issues and provide overall leadership.

Third, investigate the solutions. The greatest significance of philosophy lies in defining clear principles, determining the direction to take and inspiring mental roadmaps. The ultimate objectives of the ancient people in investigating things to extend existing knowledge are self-cultivation, leading the family, governing the country and ruling the world. Investigating solutions requires us to keep an open mind as we seek the truth based on facts; it requires us to investigate established methods for solving different contradictions, and to create new ones; it requires us to rely on both direct and indirect experience and, in the process, listen to the opinions of others as we measure these against our own personal practices. To sum it up, philosophy can sharpen our minds, broaden our vision, and give us more creative ideas.

Descartes' four-point method for investigating issues is a very valuable reference for us: The first is the rule of self-evidence; that is, unless I can confirm that something is true, I won't accept it as being true. In relation to us as accountants, a clear understanding is obtained through audit analysis and through direct observation and direct experience, not from the explanation of others or our own imagination. The second is the rule of analysis, which requires that, as far as possible, we break the problem down into its constituent parts. For example, we might be faced with trying to determine exactly why an enterprise was particularly profitable in a given year. This would involve analyzing factors attributable to the enterprise itself, as well as factors connected with politics, the economy, foreign affairs and international trends. These need to be dissected one by one, until we arrive at the most basic component. This will enable us to analyze the problem thoroughly. Then, the third rule—the rule of consolidation— is applied. By drawing together and organizing all the results of your analyses, you will find that the complex has become increasingly clear and transparent. This process of unraveling the integrated nature of knowledge was described by the French philosopher Jacques Maritain as "beginning with the experiences from the physical world and ending with the experiences of the thinker."

Descartes' fourth method is the rule of enumeration. In our case, after we have analyzed and consolidated the issues, we will need to perform an examination and audit that is completely without gaps. For example, we will highlight a few practical examples to illustrate and confirm the matter.

Conscientiously study the history of philosophy. Philosophy is developed and enriched along with the continual improvement of mankind's objective understanding of the world. It is unlike learning a scientific discipline where we do not need to study its history, because all the achievements of a scientific discipline are found within the latest developments of the discipline, and we merely need to learn and apply those. In other words, the knowledge of general disciplines is contained within the current body of knowledge, which is the sum of knowledge accumulated over a long period of time. It is different with philosophy. The manifestation of "knowledge" in philosophy is the continual quest for wisdom and the un-satiated appetite of the spirit. It is not a result of simple accumulation, but exists within the history and development of philosophy. Therefore, if we do not learn the history, we will never be able to master the discipline.

How, then, can we master the history of philosophy?

- **First, study the original works.** When we study the history of philosophy, we must study the original works, and cannot rely fully on philosophical stories or second-hand materials. You must treat the philosopher's problems as your own. You must not view them as dead items, but, if you are to understand them, treat them as having vibrant living essence filled with rich significance.

- **Second, get to the root of things.** The study of the history of philosophy is not simply knowing who the philosophers were and what they said. More importantly, we need to investigate how and why they arrived at the conclusions they did and why they said the things they said. This is the only way that we can begin to understand the essence or inner spirit behind a philosopher's thinking.

- **Third, emphasize "dialogue."** The study of the history of philosophy is a study of the philosophers' thinking along the history of philosophy. In this, we must engage our own thinking process as we analyze their thoughts. From this "dialogue" between thoughts emerges a series of self-reflections, which can serve as a means for us to discover our own gaps, understand our directions and obtain the key to solving the problem with which we are faced.

- **Fourth, open up the worldview.** This involves understanding the economic, social and historical background as well as the background of the cultural ideologies created by philosophical thought. This is the "worldview" of the philosophers, and is the basis for enabling us to understand why these thoughts or theories have been created. Perhaps we may not always truly understand the foundation for the philosophers' thoughts, but once we open up the "worldview," we may begin to understand the principle that philosophy is both a summary and the creator of the spirit of the times.

For the Chinese people, the study of philosophy particularly requires us to learn well the developmental history of Marxist philosophy. From utopian socialism to scientific socialism, from the Paris Commune to the October Revolution and then to the victory of the new democratic revolution in China, from Lenin's new economic theory to the Chinese-style socialism and then to the scientific outlook on development, Marxist philosophy was generated, enriched and refined in the midst of social development and turbulence.

In the former Soviet Union, Lenin broke away from the Marxist theory that socialism could only succeed in the most developed capitalist countries, and enabled socialism to be realized in a weak link in the capitalist chain. He created a new theory—Leninism—the core of which is leadership by the communist party to implement the people's democratic dictatorship,[6] and made use of a new economic theory—the use of the capitalist method of production to develop a socialist economy. In our country, the socialist revolution has experienced many twists and turns, and the Marxist philosophy has been supplemented and improved by the Mao Zedong Thoughts, which has led us to victory. However, in the process of constructing socialism, we were premature and hasty in adopting socialism and communism,[7] which held back our country's economic construction for a period of time. Now we have returned to the basis of seeking truth based on facts, in order to gain a new understanding of and put into practice the tenets that are put forth by the Central Communist Party regarding the construction of Chinese-style socialism. We have walked through an "S" path in the process of the socialist revolution, and we have walked an "S" path again in the process of the construction of socialism, and the common point in both of these detours is the excessive damage caused by leftism and feudalism.

Before we move on from this point, I'd like to leave you with a question to ponder. It was a question raised by the teacher in a class I was attending in the Party school: What are the similarities and differences between the initial phase of socialism and the new democratic revolution?

The many thoughts and ideas generated in the developmental history of philosophy have consciously and subconsciously dominated our actions, theories and thoughts in accounting. Since the Sixteenth CPC National Congress, the construction of a harmonious society has become a central trend of mainstream thinking in contemporary China. The role of the accountancy profession is crucial to this process as it moves forward in coordination with social, economic, cultural, environmental and legal development.

As leading talents in accounting, we need to make adequate preparation for the depth and breadth of thinking required in order to improve and enrich ourselves. We must learn and understand the history of philosophical development. Only in this way can we continuously improve and enrich our wisdom and insights, and mould our innovative capabilities and courage. We will look at the details and directions of accounting thought from a cultural and ideological perspective, and we will enrich ourselves in both the cultural and ideological domains, after which (to quote Mencius) "our spirits will be inspired, our character will be strengthened and our abilities will be greatly increased."

Perhaps we can invite geologists, biologists, anthropologists, philosophers and historians to the leading talents' training program to share their knowledge with you, so that you can all have a direct understanding of the state of the world and its developmental pathways. Through the study of history, I hope that all of you can answer the following questions: At this point in time, what position does this space and profession have in the timeline of history and in the vast universe? What indications have been obtained from the developmental process of history in relation to our thoughts, methods and perspectives? How should we sum up ourselves, learn from other people, improve ourselves and plan for the future?

Accurate understanding of the individual. The *Manifesto of the Communist Party* contains the following statement: "The free development of each individual is a condition for the free development of all people." This describes the relationship between communality and individuality. If the spirit behind this statement is applied to the training of accounting talent, we might be able to put it this way: "The growth of champions of accountancy is the basis for the joint progress of the multitude of accountants in the accountancy profession." I am not saying this to inflate your egos. Let's all think about it. In the initial stages after liberation our country had only around 200,000 people with an undergraduate degree. Just before the Cultural Revolution we had approximately two million undergraduate degree holders, and in the initial phase of economic reform and opening up, we had only about five million. What about now? Our country has 60 to 70 million people with at least an undergraduate degree! This has already exceeded the total number of people in the workforce in Japan! It is forecast that by 2020, this will have grown to 150 million, a number exceeding the total number of people in the workforce in the United States today! Such a huge batch of high-quality talent provides the strongest support for the view that China will stand proudly at the peak of the global community! It may also be one of the biggest reasons behind the real fear that some countries have towards China.

Currently, our country has one million new accounting graduates every year, from whom we should have at least a few hundred superstars each year. The responsibility of the Ministry of Finance is to select those who have the quality to become leaders, accelerate their progress, develop their potential and create the bright future of the accountancy profession. This is why I say that we need to pay attention to the collective body, but we need to pay even more attention to the individual, and we need to use the individual to develop, strengthen and enrich the collective body.

Combining the exploration of accounting issues with the study of philosophy. In the reform and development of accounting, we should investigate accounting issues from the "big-picture," value-oriented and thinking-oriented perspectives of philosophy.

- **Accounting innovation.** In the conceptual framework of philosophy, men will always perceive the objective world through a certain method. Accounting makes use of monetary measurement and financial reporting to reflect the activities of economic operations. When the functions of accounting can be transformed from auditing and reporting to control and supervision, the method in which accounting reflects economic activities will correspondingly transform from a single-value form into a scientific management form. In this sense, truth is manifested in many aspects. This explains the importance of innovation in accounting. Accounting innovation is not merely the generation of new concepts, but also includes the generation of new methods and human talent.

Accounting needs to break away from its current limitations as a measuring tool for the purposes of auditing and bookkeeping, and extend its vision into the broader realms of international rules and economic protection. The starting point of accounting theory is to broaden the basic assumptions of accounting. I am currently considering whether we can introduce the macroscopic concept of "accounting ecology" into the original foundations, and position values and traditional methodologies of accounting against the overall economic, social and industrial backdrop. It could be said that accounting has been serving the economy according to the rules and systems laid down during the 1980s and 1990s. Now, in the twenty-first century we must follow the examples of the internationalization of the Chinese economy and the globalization of the Chinese culture in influencing the entire spectrum of the capital market, social economics and international rules. Therefore, accounting needs not only to become more professional and operate according to new standards and rules, but to gain a foothold in society and the international domain, and permeate other industries and other domains in society with its professional spirit, concepts and demeanor, and to influence and change international rules and practices.

- **The generation of new accounting methods.** This is the main form of accounting innovation. The reform and development of accounting requires three forces: Maintaining the inherent driving force of accounting in the capital market, expanding the permeation of accounting into everyday life, and increasing the influence of accounting in economic operations and State policies. We need a more comprehensive, timely, direct and effective collection of basic information in economic activities to ensure the veracity of accounting reports. This will elevate accounting from its traditional bookkeeping function and give it integrated analysis and forecasting functions for wider economic and social reform.

For example, during the age of manual bookkeeping, the collection of accounting information could not be done in great detail because of the cost implications and a provision shop could adopt the weighted average or simple average method to record its inventory costs. Now, in the digital age, every product in a large supermarket has its own code, making it possible to keep track of every incoming and outgoing item and obviating the need to make use of the weighted average. Further illustrations of how technology can be used to bring innovations include Sinopec's introduction of a centralized audit method that used a common software platform to resolve the gaps of time and space in its accounting treatment; or the introduction by the Administrative Fee Management Centre of the Hainan Province Finance Department of a horizontal centralized payment system which is able to provide timely feedback on the revenues, expenditures and surpluses of its scores of subsidiaries, and increase the utilization rate of funds; or the provision by Hubei Province of centralized accounting treatment services which enable auditing across both the horizontal administrative agencies and the vertical village groups. The generation of these new accounting methods shows the potential for accounting to expand its significance and value. We need to carry out effective research and promotion of this area.

- **The generation of new accounting talents.** During the CPA leading talents' training program, I said that you need to become a banner, a torch and a seed for the profession. You need to become the face of the profession and provide leadership; you need to be a torch and provide influence; and you need to be a seed and develop the latent potential. You as individuals can improve things for the wider community.

The values of accounting. Accounting must not only seek the truth, but must also strive for goodness and for beauty. "Goodness" refers to the integrity of accounting; "beauty" refers to the quality of accounting. In the course of overall economic and social development, accountants are equivalent to linesmen in an athletics event and scorers in a shooting event. If linesmen and scorers cheat, how can the competition be conducted in a fair manner? How can the credibility of the competition be established? Therefore accountants, particularly leading talents in the profession, must certainly cultivate good moral character and strong integrity. In relation to issues of accounting integrity, we must pay attention to the construction of both the system and the culture, strengthening professional conduct through the system and softening values of accountants through culture.

I have said previously that accountants need to have strength of character like the bamboo. This is true, but we also need to have the qualities of jade, which remains pure and unblemished even in a bad environment. We must also have a mild disposition but have the inner strength to resist improper instructions, even when pressure is applied. We must have the courage to protect the interests of society, and have a weighing scale within our hearts to weigh the degree of importance of the issues. As qualified accountants, we must place the law above our superiors and adhere only to the law.

The development of accounting language. Philosophy and language are closely related fields. Behind the development and movement of every language, we can definitely see the influence of the philosophy of the times. Linguists tell us that people live among a series of linguistic codes, and the only connection between people and the world is the linguistic code. To the philosopher, language is the carrier of human life. Accounting language functions as the code that connects accounting with the socioeconomic world and the lives of people, and should continue to be remolded and elevated to a higher level within the modern conceptions of philosophy.

The language of accounting is inherently complex and is not easily understood by the general public. I have been giving this a great deal of thought in relation to the computer interface, where the hardware can be very sophisticated, and the application software can be very complex, but the interface is displayed in such a way that it is very user-friendly. To apply this to the language of accounting would require that the language is changed to suit the tastes of the target audience, in much the same way that Zhang Yimou makes his movies accessible to foreign as well as to Chinese audiences. Currently, accounting language can only be understood by experts with a very strong background of professional knowledge. Actually, it is entirely possible to express complex economic activities in simple terminology that will enable ordinary investors and the general public to understand the subject.

Accounting does not have the fireworks created in the "audit storm,"[8] and does not draw as much attention as the country's economic statistics. The problem that we face currently is that though accounting has done a lot of work, it rarely has a voice of its own. This is largely because traditional accountants only know how to explain accounts using accounting language, and there is no interaction and empathy with the other disciplines. How then can we transform the language of accounting into a language that can be understood by society at large? Here we have an example of the limitations of knowledge, of thinking and of perspectives working against the profession. In many circumstances, thinking has been "formatted" by accounting, and vision has been confined within the view from a fixed window. Now is the time for us to re-package the system. Language originally existed to make it convenient for people to communicate with each other and facilitate the transmission of information. It is only by making accounting language more accessible to the general public that it can be more easily understood and applied by people who are not professional accountants and more easily provide services to the socioeconomic and political domain.

A grand vision of the future of accounting. The essence of philosophy is the unity of opposites, of communality and individuality. If all the accountants are the community, then the highly-talented accountants are the individualities that exist within such a group. As Hu Angang, who is an influential economics professor in the School of Public Policy and Management at Tsinghua University and an advocate of "green revolution," has pointed out, when we invest in the training of champions of accountancy, we are investing in the future of accounting. Currently there are over 12 million accountants in China, but only around 300 leading accounting talents, and these are still undergoing training, and cannot be considered as real leading talents yet. This ratio of approximately 40,000 to one is too big, and there are too few champions. In *The Romance of the Three Kingdoms*, Cao Cao is described as having a huge army with many generals, and it is often said that "for every million valiant soldiers, there are a thousand generals." In our current situation, there are 12 million valiant soldiers and only a few hundred generals. The ancients had the following saying: "Life becomes free from doubts at 40." But how applicable is this within our profession? Are all our comrades who are 40 years old able to lead China's accountancy profession out into the world? Only when we have accumulated a certain number of talents who are free from doubt can we effectively promote the production quality of accounting in China to move forward. If we add two more zeros to the numbers of the leading accounting talents that we currently have, and further develop fully the various accounting elites who are currently talents in the various industries, it would be like the image of "an army with golden spears and armored horses swallowing up thousands of miles like the tiger!"[9]

We can look forward to a day when the training and selection of leading accounting talents will not require the intervention of the government and the industry organization. We can then do away with training programs such as this to select and train leading talents in accounting because they will be produced naturally and will emerge on their own. With so much talent at their disposal, the Accounting Society of China, the China Association of Chief Financial Officers and the Chinese Institute of Certified Public Accountants (CICPA) would step up another notch and that will be the moment that the accountancy profession in China flourishes and soars.

HOW TO APPLY PHILOSOPHY EFFECTIVELY

Since the winter of 2005, we have made a pact to "make noble character and integrity as our foundation and to give priority to understanding the essence of the profession," and we also encouraged each other to "maintain high ethical standards while we skillfully perform to our abilities." We have explored the pathways by which an operative is transformed into a manager, leader and strategist, all the while aspiring to innovative thinking and the pursuit of excellence! As champions of accountancy, all of you should conscientiously abide by the objectives of the human resource training objectives, overcome difficulties, strive to be molded, be faithful in your mission, and be courageous in assuming the responsibilities of creating the brilliant future of the accountancy profession in China. In exploring how to apply philosophical problems, the following points should be particularly noted.

A balanced perspective in distinguishing right from wrong. Balance is the core principle of the system of measurement in accounting, and is the cornerstone of the balance sheet. If the accounts are not balanced there must be an error somewhere. Imbalance is not acceptable in accounting. Even if a single cent is missing, it is necessary to look through the books, check the receipts and, if necessary, burn the midnight oil in search of the missing cent. However, in life we favor one over another, and violate the principles of balance. The daily accumulation of such imbalances would cause our lives to be in disarray and confusion. Therefore we need to bring the concept of balance from the abacus beads of accounting into our everyday lives, into the social relationships of respect for elders and love for children, into life planning, and into the harmonious and scientific development of political governance. To put it simply, there must be a measuring scale in our hearts, and we need to stress the importance of balance in both big things and small things. There can be harmony only when there is balance, without which we will not realize our objectives.

Understanding cause and effect. If it is said that balance is the cornerstone of the balance sheet, then matching is the soul of the profit and loss statement. Traditional accounting theory takes the view that matching includes the matching of time and the matching of cause and effect. Actually the matching of time is only an expression of the matching of cause and effect, which is the core of the matching principle. The rules of cause and effect have been comprehensively implemented in accounting, and this has confirmed the scientific foundation of the accounting discipline. Accountants are familiar with using the matching principle in handling accounting matters, but should further apply this concept to their work and lives. Some people may seek to obtain huge returns from minimal investments, and end up with short-term pleasures but long-term problems. Such erroneous thinking needs to be corrected through the effective use of the matching principle in accounting.

Knowing when to advance and when to retreat. The principle of conservatism is a reflection of the unique perspective from which accounting views the world: Prevention is better than cure; talent and beauty are hidden. In an age of public display of individuality and impulsive behavior, many people lack this type of accounting concept. The principle of conservatism inspires us not be carried away with success, and to make preparations for retreat when we are advancing, and to conserve potential energy during low tides for when the tide is high. Accounting statements that are directed by the principle of conservatism display an internal beauty that is natural and needs no cosmetics. Similarly, under the direction of this principle, joy and anger in life are displayed only in moderation, and the individual knows when it is appropriate to advance or retreat.

Understand fairness and practice impartiality. "Fairness" is another major facet of accounting theory. In the gradual pursuit of truth, if we cannot achieve absolute truth, at least there is still relative fairness. The principle of fairness nimbly brings democratic concepts into the technical practice of accounting measurements. In determining the price of an asset, the principle of fairness requires us to find the value in a fair trade between two parties who are fully apprised of the circumstances and who voluntarily carry out an exchange of assets or settlement of debt. Fair trade, being fully apprised of the circumstances, and voluntary actions constitute the main characteristics of the principle of fairness, and also provide a very good system of reference in our dealings with others. If we can achieve these three points, then even in the most complex matters we will be able to find a solution that is universally accepted, and achieve "fairness." Failure to achieve them, on the other hand, will inevitably give rise to conflict and will not produce a solution no matter how hard you try.

Leading talents must pay attention to developing their philosophical cultivation, stepping beyond the technical boundaries of accounting to observe spiritual factors such as the ecology, values and qualities of accounting. They must not only be able to distinguish right from wrong by applying theoretical rules, but also be able to come up with new ideas, new rules for telling right from wrong devised from practical application in the real world.

This requires a broader vision and deeper wisdom that might be manifest in both the practical realm—in the quest to eliminate forgery, say—and in establishing trends that seek to remove confusion through achieving a clear understanding of ourselves and others, of individuality and communality, of the present and the future, and of relatives and absolutes. Here "others" does not refer to individuals, but to the accounting entity, discipline and profession. Many people are accustomed to esteeming themselves above others and benefiting themselves at the expense of others. The consolidated reports in accounting and the theory of responsibility centers have broken through the absolute limits of accounting entities vis-à-vis others, such that subsidiaries, enterprise groups, and even an entire profession, a country or the entire world can now be viewed as an accounting entity. For example, in accounting terms, global warming is similar to a deferred debit that occurs when the entire planet is viewed as a complete accounting entity, and if we do not settle it in a timely manner, after a long period of accumulation, it could result in disaster.

At the same time the accounting entity can also be much smaller units—a workshop, a team and even a worker or a product. Similarly, the drawing up of boundaries between the accounting discipline and other disciplines and between the accountancy profession and other industries is like the demarcation of the borders for the accounting entity, and is full of relativity and multiplicity. This creates a huge conflict with the traditional self-centered value system, and also brings about a strong challenge to the system for evaluating accounting information. Leading talents must be able to confront these problems and challenges directly, and achieve success through hard work.

Leading accounting talents have the potential to promote the scientific development of accounting matters, to gain full understanding through deep contemplation, to observe the truth and continually move towards the human ideal that was expressed by the philosopher Zhang Hengqu, from the Northern Song dynasty: "Establishing the core for heaven and earth, establishing life for the people, continuing the teachings of the saints and bringing peace to the world."

In concluding my preliminary understandings, thoughts and experiences in relation to philosophical problems, I would like to emphasize that philosophy is a container of the human spirit, and we can capture from within it the human spirit and trajectory and trends in human history. Learning philosophy is not an end in itself. The crucial principle is that through philosophical contemplation, we can grasp the spirit of the times from a macroscopic perspective. Through understanding the objective trends for the reform and development of accounting, and thereby further understanding the scientific worldviews and methodologies, and through improving our own strategic thinking ability and intellectual and ethical qualities, we will enable the accounting profession to be effective in servicing the economic development of the socialist market.

The internationalization of the accountancy profession in China has just started. I hope that along the path of accounting reform and development, all of us will ride through the storms, unite together, and contribute our utmost abilities and wisdom, to realize one breakthrough after another, and to scale one new peak after another.

ENDNOTES

1 Edited version of the speech given at the Second Joint Training Session of National (Prospective) Leading Accounting Talents, September 29, 2007.

2 Also called the *I Ching*, this is one of the oldest of the Chinese classic texts. The book contains a divination system comparable to Western geomancy or the West African Ifá system. In Western cultures and modern East Asia, it is still widely used for this purpose.

3 Feng Youlan or Fung Yu-Lan (1895–1990) is known mostly for his books *New Rational Philosophy and History of Chinese Philosophy*. An original and influential philosopher, he played an important role in reintroducing the study of Chinese philosophy.

4 Lǐ Ruìhuán (September 1934–), a former state leader of China. He was a member of the Standing Committee of the Political Bureau of the Fifteenth Central Committee of the Communist Party of China until November 2002. He served as Chairman of the Ninth National

Committee of the Chinese People's Political Consultative Conference (CPPCC) until March 2003.

5 From the *Doctrine of Mean*, one of the Four Books of the Confucian canonical scriptures. The purpose of the book is to demonstrate the usefulness of a golden way to gain perfect virtue.

6 The premise of the "people's democratic dictatorship" is that the ruling party and the state democratically represent and act on behalf of the people, but possess and may use dictatorial powers against reactionary forces. In Chinese, the word "dictatorship" does not necessarily have negative connotation, being dissociated from the concepts that are closest to the Western *dictator*.

7 This is a reference to the Great Leap Forward, an economic and social plan used from 1958 to 1961, which aimed to use China's vast population to rapidly transform China from an agrarian economy into a modern communist society through agricultural reform and industrialization. It ended in catastrophe as it triggered a widespread famine that resulted in tens of millions of deaths.

8 "Audit storm" was a phrase coined by the Chinese media to describe the auditing campaigns initiated by the National Audit Office of China. In 2003, Auditor General Li Jinhua presented the annual audit report to the Standing Committee of the National People's Congress. He openly disclosed the severe irregularities committed by many ministries and other government agencies. This report was posted on the official NAO website, the first time that an audit report had been made public. This received considerable public attention. In July 2004, "audit storm" was voted one of the 10 most popular terms used in Chinese newspapers in the spring and summer of that year.

9 Lines from a poem by Xin Qiji (1140–1207), a poet of the Southern Song Dynasty.

Chapter 8

Studying Classics for Enlightenment[1]

The report of the Sixteenth National Congress of the Communist Party of China (CPC), while elaborating on the lofty objectives of building a well-off society, states that "to promote comprehensive human development, it is important to form a learning society where everyone learns throughout their lifetime." The report of the Seventeenth CPC National Congress reiterates that "it is important to build a learning society where everyone learns throughout their lifetime." It is therefore essential to gain a full understanding of the importance of learning from a holistic perspective.

What is an outstanding individual? Different people may have different opinions, but I think that the most important point is that the individual must be an intellectual. People often say that Tao originates from quietness, morality from humility, benevolence from philanthropy, kindness from gratitude, fortune from happiness, and pleasure from health. Then, where does intellect come from? I think that intellect comes from erudition. As the Buddhist scriptures tell us: "Erudition helps one acquire knowledge, steer clear of viciousness, get rid of nonsense, and attain Nirvana." To be erudite, it is essential to read as many good books as possible and apply what you have learned. By reading, we can enrich and elevate ourselves, enlighten our minds, and acquire Tao. A good book, irrespective of its age, thickness and subject matter, is always an embodiment of precious spiritual wealth, and none more so than the classics.

WHAT ARE THE CLASSICS?

In ancient Chinese, the word for "classics" consisted of two characters, *jing* and *dian*. *Jing* derived from the character signifying "longitude." This later became applied to time to indicate "linking up and extending history" and also came to mean "constant." By the time of the Eastern Han Dynasty it was associated with a respected body of literature whose constant ways and grand teachings transcended time. *Dian* literally mean a big volume and represents important books. The word *jing dian* applied to books which set out unchanging principles and rules, and was gradually extended to incorporate other fields of art, culture and natural science and became a generic word for authoritative volumes. Thus today, classics are books of outstanding merit that have been passed down through the generations and never fail to enlighten readers.

I believe that classics exhibit the following characteristics:

Originality: The work is essentially a new creation, rather than an imitation or an expansion of something already in existence. Classics are original, which generally means that the creator has opened up one or more new fields with creative thinking or action, and therefore embodies an unprecedented societal consciousness, humanistic realm, time content, scientific level and technical standard. For example, *The History of the Peloponnesian War* by Thucydides, hailed as the first global general history book, was the first book to use the narrative style to relate history. Euclid's *Elements* has the distinction of being the world's first mathematical book with a rigorous theory and complete system, and its role in the development of mathematics largely remains unparalleled even today. *Institutiones* by Gaius is considered the only surviving complete book on ancient Roman law and is the foundation and model for all civil codes around the world. *A Treatise of Taxes and Contributions* by William Petty was the first book to conscientiously attribute the value of commodities to labor. *The Wealth of Nations* by Adam Smith was the world's first systematic analysis and account of socioeconomic life, and is universally recognized as the foundation of modern Western economics. Einstein's *On the Electrodynamics of Moving Bodies* was the first scientific elaboration on the principle of relativity in its narrow sense.

In China, books classified as classics are all original. For instance, *The Book of Poetry* was the first poetry anthology, *Shangshu* was the first collection of essays, *The Analects of Confucius* was China's first quotation-style collection of essays, *National Language* was China's first country-specific history book, *Zuozhuan* was the first chronological history book with complete narration, *Historical Record* was the first general history book presented in a series of biographies, and *The Book of Han* was the first dynastic history book presented in a series of biographies. It is clear that in both China and the rest of the world, all classics were pioneers in their times and have endured the test of time to become cultural masterpieces. They are the embodiment of the essence of the times, the intellect of society, and the creation of genius; they represent a new way of observing things and analyzing problems; they transcend traditional theories, existing knowledge, and outdated methodologies and systems.

Culture: Culture generally refers to the sum total of the spiritual wealth created by man in the process of socioeconomic development. The classics have a significance beyond their specific field and are underpinned by—and, in turn, extend and promote—their cultural heritage. They are rooted in culture; culture spawns new classics. Culture without classics is no culture; likewise, classics without culture are no classics. Classics emerge in quick succession as culture prospers, and culture spreads farther and exerts a long-lasting influence as classics are disseminated. The essence of human civilization lies in the depth of classics. Human civilization would not have been sustained but for the continuous stream of classics. If the top 50 classic books in each field were missing, the world of the human spirit would be plunged into darkness. We simply cannot imagine what Western civilization would have been like without Dante, Homer, Plato, Aristotle, Leonardo da Vinci, Michelangelo, Shakespeare, Goethe, Beethoven, Mozart, Van Gogh, Picasso and many other classic personages. Similarly, it is hard to imagine what Chinese civilization would have become if there had not been classic books such as *The Book of Changes*, *The Book of Poetry*, *Historical Record*, *The Book of Han*, *A Dream of Red Mansions*, and *The Romance of Three Kingdoms*, and classic personages such as Confucius, Mencius, Li Bai, Du Fu, Han Yu, Su Shi, Wang Xizhi, Gu Kaizhi, Wu Daozi and the like.

If Galileo had not conducted the free-fall experiment at the Leaning Tower of Pisa, humankind would not have been able to understand the real nature of gravitational force and gravity so early or to negate, in both practice and theory, Aristotle's "Motion and the Law of Falling Bodies," which had dominated the scientific community for more than a thousand years. Without these, science would not have developed so rapidly in modern times and human civilization would not be what it is today.

Radiation: This concept in physics has been borrowed by the social sciences to mean extensive influence beyond the constraints of time and space. The radiating nature of classics is evident first of all in the significant influence they exert in the relevant field or directly related fields. *The Art of War* by Sun Tzu, for example, is not only a book on military strategy, but has become classic reading for tactical guidance of all kinds. The book's military philosophy has exerted a profound influence in China's military throughout history and has transcended national borders, being translated into 29 languages, including Japanese, English, French, German, and Russian. As evidence of how avidly it is read around the world, on a visit to China in September 1961, British General Field Marshal Bernard Montgomery, the renowned Commander of the Allied Forces in the Second World War, recommended that it be adopted as a textbook for military academies worldwide. Indeed, many military academies have done exactly that. It is reported that during the Gulf War in 1991, both sides studied *The Art of War*, hoping to gain an edge.

Newton's *Principia Mathematica* is indisputably an epic work in both the history of science and the history of human civilization. It represents humankind's first complete and scientific theory of the universe and a system of scientific theories; its influence can be felt in all fields of classical natural sciences. Within the field of scientific research, it is also a model for the modern system of scientific theories, involving various aspects of the structure of theory systems, research methodologies and approaches, and the relationship between man and nature. Einstein's comment about Newton's work—that " . . . all achievements we have obtained to date would not have been possible"—confirm its importance. Even today, the problems and solutions discussed in the *Principia* remain part of the key content of mathematics and science programs at universities, contributing to the intellectual growth of generations of young people and driving human science and society forward.

In our own field of accounting and auditing, works such as *An Introduction to Corporate Accounting Standards* by William Andrew Paton and A. C. Littleton, *Handbook of Modern Accounting* by Sidney Davidson, *Accounting Theory* by Eldon S. Hendriksen, *Positive Accounting Theory* by Ross L. Watts, and *Montgomery's Auditing* by Robert H. Montgomery have exerted an immeasurable influence on the development of theory and practice. It is precisely because of the scientific absorption of these classics that China's research on modern accounting and auditing theories and related education has been able to emerge from the disruption and disorientation of the Cultural Revolution and contribute to China's socioeconomic reform and international development.

The radiating nature of classics is also manifested in the tremendous influence they have on unrelated fields. For example, *The Art of War* is not only influential in the military arena; it is also considered to be a classical work by statesmen, thinkers and entrepreneurs. *The Book of Changes*, an ancient classic philosophical work in China which studies heaven and earth, explores the universe, provides guidance on life, and advises on careers, reaches far beyond the realm of philosophy. The book was used extensively in ancient China in a wide range of fields, such as history, politics, military matters, mathematics, and medicine. Most of China's prehistoric and pre-Qin records are documents on divination using the Eight Diagrams. Renowned military strategists Sun Bin and Zhuge Liang both used the Eight Diagrams in deploying their troops and gained tremendous victories. *The Book of Changes* has also guided and driven the development of diagnosis in traditional Chinese medicine and the prediction of diseases. Its role has been variously described as authoritative in China's political and military fields; dominating in the economic field; innovative in practice; informative, interesting and practical in the cultural and scientific fields; and instrumental in decision-making in life. In fact, such traditional philosophical classics have also exerted a significant influence on the development of human science. Gottfried Leibnitz, the German mathematician and a forerunner of modern science, once applied the principle of the Fuxi Eight Diagrams in inventing the binary system which was later adopted in modern computers. Ilya Prigogine, the winner of the 1977 Nobel Prize in Chemistry, summed up the influence of Chinese thinking this way: "The development of new modern sciences and the research in physics and mathematics in the last 10 years . . . all conform more to China's philosophical thinking . . . For Western scientists, Chinese thinking is always a source of inspiration."

Profoundness: Profoundness typically refers to a work's depth and its ability to touch upon the real nature of an issue. Classics are the crystallization of wisdom and the refinement of knowledge; at the same time, they are the concentration and distillation of the spirits and emotions of the wise, the perceptive world, logical reasoning, and scientific experimentation. They reproduce, perceive and describe the truth of, and relations among, things, between things and nature and society, between things and related and non-related parties, and the rules of such relations. *The Analects of Confucius*, for instance, is a classical work on Confucian thought; it is a grand collection of Chinese culture since ancient times, involving the politics, education, history, life, philosophy and religion of ancient China. The wisdom contained in the book continues to amaze people today. It is marked by an ability to lay bare the truth with a single remark. On the methods of learning it says, "Learning without thinking means labor lost; thinking without learning is perilous." On enthusiasm for work, it says: "To merely know something is nothing compared to being interested in doing something; being interested in doing something is nothing compared to deriving joy from doing it." These oft-quoted classical quotations of life and wisdom derive from an insight into matters. They belong both to China and to the world at large, gaining acceptance among all human beings. Among the conclusions of the first international convention of Nobel Prize-winners, held in Paris in 1988, was one stating that "if humankind is to continue to survive, it must go back 25 centuries to draw upon the wisdom of Confucius."

Zizhi Tongjian (*Comprehensive Mirror to Aid in Government*), written by Sima Guang of the Northern Song Dynasty and published in the form of a chronicle, is the most voluminous and sophisticated reference work in Chinese historiography. The book took 19 years to complete and covered a period of 1,326 years. It provided a chronological account of the relations among politics, the military and nations and commented on economy, culture, academic thought and historical figures. Hailed by subsequent generations as the ultimate guidebook on practical knowledge on managing state affairs, it had simple wording but was incisive and pertinent.

As mentioned earlier, Adam Smith's *The Wealth of Nations* is widely considered the foundation of modern Western economics, and has had a profound influence on the economy, politics and culture of the Western world. It focuses on the generation and distribution of wealth and elaborates on theories covering such matters as the division of labor, currencies, commodity value and price, wages and profits, capital accumulation, and the theory of state, thereby building a relatively complete system of theories on market economy. The British used the book to promote free trade and build a global market, eventually realizing their dream of becoming a great power.

Adam Smith's other monumental classic, *The Theory of Moral Sentiments*, though eclipsed somewhat by *The Wealth of Nations*, is considered by many to be as important in that it was the first ever book to provide a comprehensive and systematic analysis of human emotions. This landmark book laid out the view that the pursuit of material interests should be constrained by moral sentiments that refrained from hurting others but, rather, helped them. This "altruistic" moral sentiment should remain deep-seated in the soul of humankind forever; moreover, the creation and maintenance of such unaffected sentiment by everyone is essential for the harmonious development of the entire market economy and even for the prosperity of a nation. Renowned economist Milton Friedman aptly commented that before reading *The Wealth of Nations* he had no idea what egoism was, and that it was not until after reading *The Theory of Moral Sentiments* that he understood that altruism meant "egoism with a clear conscience."

In the accounting field, works which shed light on and provide a profound summary of the composition and internal rules of the system of accounting theories have all become highly influential accounting classics. Such works include *The Structure of Accounting Theory* by A. C. Littleton, *The Philosophy of Auditing* by R. K. Mautz and H. A. Sharaf, and the financial accounting conceptual framework established by the US Financial Accounting Standards Board.

Evergreen: The classics are frequently read and frequently referred to. They are able to survive repeated testing and are useful in taking stock of the past, guiding the present, and foreseeing the future. The tree of classics is evergreen because it is rooted in fertile soil and because it contemplates and expounds upon the fundamental issues of human survival and development, nature and many other fields in a unique and unparalleled manner. Classics exceed the realm and constraints of the specific practice of the time and exert far-reaching rational implications; their depth, breadth, and areas of spiritual growth hold enduring interest for future generations. They have stood the test of time and repeated investigation. In a new environment, they never fail to unleash fresh energy, stimulate fresh thinking, and spawn new research fields and disciplines. For example, Darwin's *On the Origin of Species* not only laid the scientific foundation for the theory of evolution, but continues to play a significant role in guiding contemporary research on the origin of organisms, the division of species, and genetics. Einstein's *Theory of Relativity* has not only laid the foundation for modern physics, but is also extensively used in research on nuclear physics, nanotechnology, space and aeronautics; no one can tell how this theory will continue to affect our future life.

Poetry, too, can fall into the classical category. For example, Li Bai's *In the Still of the Night* ("Abed, I see a silver light, I wonder if it is frost aground. Looking up, I find the moon bright; bowing, in homesickness I'm drowned.") has exerted a lasting influence over many generations of readers. A simple tale of a traveler's homesickness, its message continues to reverberate in many hearts. I first came across the poem when I was a child and it stirred me then, even before I had experienced fully the emotions it expressed. Subsequently, when I was away from my home and parents at university, or, later, receiving "re-education" in the countryside or later still when I began my career in Beijing—and even today—the poem evokes powerful feelings of longing and nostalgia and yet has the power to soothe those strong emotions. Like a good wine, the poem mellows with time.

In the accounting field, classic books such as *Dicksee's Auditing*, *Montgomery's Auditing* and *Kohler's Dictionary for Accountants*, despite subsequent revisions and additions by others, are widely considered to be enduring evergreen works that will always give new knowledge and fresh enlightenment. As the Italian writer Calvino put it, "Classics are the books that you often hear someone saying that 'I'm rereading them' rather than 'I'm reading them.'" Reading a classic book for the first time is, strangely, like being reunited with a long-lost friend, while rereading it is like meeting someone for the first time: There is always something fresh and new to be gained from each reading.

All of our discussion so far has been related to words. It is important to note, however, that invaluable knowledge and experience is not confined to the written word; it can come in the form of paintings, songs, photographs and videos, or from war and other major social and economic events, or from natural disasters. These too form an integral part of the treasure house of experience from which we can draw.

WHY IT IS IMPORTANT TO STUDY CLASSICS

Our beloved former Premier Zhou Enlai once admonished, "Study hard for the rise of the Chinese nation." Renowned English thinker, philosopher and politician Francis Bacon asserted: "Studies serve for delight, for ornament, and for ability . . . Histories make men wise; poets witty; the mathematics subtle; natural philosophy deep; morals grave; logic and rhetoric able to contend. *Abeunt studia in mores* [Studies pass into and influence manners]." Zeng Guofan, one of China's most eminent people in the pre-modern period, was an avid reader throughout his life. He affirmed, "The nature of humans is inborn and hard to change, except by reading." Lin Yutang[2] proclaimed that reading "enlightens the mind, eliminates prejudice, acquires new knowledge, expands learning, enriches experience, and cultivates character." All these comments are inspiring and thought-provoking. Reading general books can be helpful; studying classics is much more beneficial, as I hope to illustrate.

- **Enriching life:** To have a beautiful life, proper values must be established. Values are generally the products of the life practices and accumulated cultural heritage of a nation, a class, a social stratum or an individual. They are used as standards and principles by which to evaluate matters and persons. To establish proper values, the key is to establish proper relations with yourself, with others and with nature. This is particularly important for people in the accounting profession, who are in many ways the middle link of a chain of social relations. By establishing proper values, accounting professionals can contribute to the harmonization of all kinds of social relations from workplace to society. If they fail to do so, the entire system of social signals will be problematic. After all, as my supervising professor Yang Shizan once said to me, "If planning becomes chaotic, the world will be thrown into chaos; if planning is properly executed, the world will be in order."

Studying and contemplating classics will help us establish proper values. The key to everything is personal integrity, as Pan Xulun knew well. "Integrity," he said, "helps you set goals, stay flawless, handle matters, and manage interpersonal relations; don't forget about integrity and you will become trustworthy."

Mencius asserted that "a true man is not to be corrupted by riches or honors, depart from principles because of poverty or humble origins, or submit to force or threat." Chuang Tzu pushed for "coexistence with heaven and earth and unification with all other creatures"; in other words, he called upon people to live in harmony with all things. What a lofty realm of life this is! From here, accounting professionals at least can elevate their aspirations for safeguarding national interests and those of investors. Only in this way will they resist mundane temptations and refrain from malpractices for selfish ends and steer clear of acts of deceit and dishonesty.

To handle relations with others properly is to manage interpersonal relations, ethnic relations and group relations properly. *The Analects of Confucius* states that "to establish self, first help to establish others; to fulfill one's own achievement, first let others achieve." In other words, we are supposed to help others achieve the goals that we ourselves want to realize. At the heart of it all lies a single word—benevolence. The traditional classics tell us that we must also be courteous; to be "different yet harmonious" and to understand that "terrestrial advantages . . . are less important than the unity among people."

Regarding the way to handle relations between people and their country, the classics tell us that "all people share a responsibility for the rise and fall of their nation" and urge us to be loyal to our nation and people. As we reach out to the world and strive to bring our accounting and auditing standards into convergence with international standards, we should keep these guidelines in mind, exercising caution as we seek to achieve harmony while maintaining our national characteristics, and safeguarding our national interests.

With regard to the relationship between man and nature, Mencius advocated "examining your heart and knowing your nature until you know heaven." He believed that man had empathy with heaven and earth and was able to enter the realm of heaven and earth. Taoists also push for "unification of heaven and man" and emphasize the need to adapt to nature's changing patterns while arguing that man is not passive and can play a role in nature's changes. *The Great Legend of the Book of Changes* states that "man divides and completes the course of heaven and earth and furthers and regulates the gifts of heaven and earth" and that "man moulds and encompasses all transformations of heaven and earth without mistake, and stoops to turn things into completion without missing any." In other words, it is important to tap man's initiative to regulate the changes of nature and to assist all other creatures in attaining perfection. These insightful comments are undoubtedly very helpful for us in forming proper life values.

- **Enlightening the mind:** Although different civilizations around the world have different origins, the classics that survive from these represent the distillation of the great wisdom of humankind. The classics, which embody that wisdom, are a vast treasure house of thought that forever illuminates the minds of future generations.

Maxim Gorky admonished us to "Love reading" because "it will make your life more relaxed; it will help you sort out your chaotic thoughts, emotions and events in a friendly manner; it will teach you how to respect others and yourself; and it will inspire wisdom and the mind with affection for the world and mankind." Thus, studying classics allows us to experience a delightful journey of mental development, so that we can liberate our mind, stretch our body and soul, activate our intellectual power, and stay active in contemplating the world and our place in it. During the course of reading classics, we can have "dialogues" with classical characters and thoughts and have hearty conversations with sages of all periods. The enlightenment to be had from such conversations will enable us to gain a better understanding of man's enduring culture and history, of the vastness of the world, and how the system of great thoughts and rigorous scientific theories have been formulated, built and developed. This will not only enrich our knowledge, but also enhance our ability to observe and evaluate the world, to experience the delights of the unexpected, to taste success and happiness, and to elevate our thoughts to great heights. Moreover, it will enhance our moral state and purify our soul.

In accounting terms, if popular culture is a form of consumerism, then studying classics must be an investment. *The Art of War*, for example, contains much that is of value in planning accounting undertakings, facilitating institutional development, and overcoming difficulties and challenges on our way. The qualities it extols in consummate military leaders are equally and more broadly applicable in our profession, too. To take just a few examples: The need for knowledge ("He who knows will be victorious; he who knows not will not win"); the ability to maximize victory with minimal attrition ("In the practical art of war, the best thing of all is to take the enemy's country whole and intact; to shatter and destroy it is second best. So, too, it is better to recapture an army entirely than to destroy it, to capture a regiment, a detachment or a company entirely than to destroy them"); the ability to plan and to create the conditions for victory before engaging the enemy ("In war, the victorious strategist only seeks battle after the victory has been won, whereas he who is destined to defeat first fights and afterwards looks for victory"); the ability to use the situation and the available resources to the best advantage ("The consummate combatant looks to the effect of the situation, and does not require too much from individuals; hence his ability to pick out the right men and utilize the situation"); and the need for discipline in achieving the required ends ("The consummate leader cultivates the moral law, and strictly adheres to method and discipline; thus it is in his power to control victory and defeat")—all can be absorbed and used to great effect in working towards our ultimate goals for this profession.

The Book of Changes elaborates on the principles of the way of heaven, life, self-cultivation, family, people and state governance. It is one of the cornerstones of Chinese culture and one of the sources of inspiration for Chinese ideology and national spirit. The more we understand it, the calmer our minds will become and the wiser and more resilient we will grow.

I once wrote a short article about the peaceful rise of China as a fresh path of development in human history. Its core spirit is precisely in line with two propositions in *The Book of Changes*—"As heaven maintains vigor through movements, a gentleman should constantly strive for self-perfection. As earth's condition is receptive to devotion, a gentleman should hold the outer world with great virtues." To "constantly strive for self-perfection" means never relaxing one's efforts to advance; it reflects the Chinese nation's resilience and determination to press ahead against all odds. To "hold the outer world with great virtues" promotes tolerance for everything and, thus, harmony. This reflects the integrating, vast and tolerant nature of the harmonious thought of the Chinese nation. If we regard these attributes as coordinates, the resilience would be the longitudinal coordinates advancing China's national strength, while harmony would be the latitudinal coordinates steering the nation's development to neutrality and peace.

It's noteworthy that the "core" of classics in enlightening our minds is the "way" (*tao*) rather than the "technique" (*shu*)—direction and principles, rather than specific actions. "Way" originally meant "path" and later assumed the meaning of "principle," or the pattern of things. "Way" is a form of ideology, reflecting the fundamental nature of the world and from which all else emanates. The "technique" is behavior, and refers to what to do and how to do it. For example, how to attain something is related to the technique and what to give up and what to hold on to is about the way. In general, the "technique" lies in classical methods, formulas and paths, whereas the "way" lies within the "soul" of classics. If we can comprehend the "way" and acquire the "technique," combining and making them complementary, it will be enormously helpful in enlightening our minds.

- **Training our thinking:** Thinking is a cognitive process which involves analyzing, summarizing, judging and inferring on the basis of presentation and conception. It reflects the objective world and, in turn, acts on the subjective world through practice. The way of thinking refers to the principles, methods or approaches and measures adopted in the process of thinking. It exists throughout the process of cognition. The more flexible the way of thinking and the more it conforms with the objective rules of thinking, the more objective people's understanding will be; passivity and constraint give way to activity and freedom. Studying classics not only enlightens our minds, but also improves our way of thinking and helps us develop a scientific way of thinking.

According to *The Book of Changes*, all life can be represented by *yin* (the shadow, which is the passive, feminine principle of life) and *yang* (the sun, which is the active, masculine principle).[3] In addition to this image-based way of thinking, *The Book of Changes* also presents holistic and dialectic ways of thinking, arranging its 64 hexagrams as the opposition and unity of *yin* and *yang* and the alternation and mutual compensation of the rigid and the flexible. This holistic way of thinking also puts forward various antitheses, such as the sun and the moon, and winter and summer, which are in a dynamic flux driven by "mutual interaction" and "mutual perception" and in which the antitheses are in collision and in reciprocal extrapolation, giving rise to change. The tendency of the flux is "to go to extremes"— when the paradox reaches its pinnacle, it changes to its opposite. The result of such a change is the creation of the cyclic theory focused on "repetition revealing the heart of heaven and earth." How brilliant is this dialectic way of thinking! I cannot help but marvel at the use of a mere 64 diagrams to capture all objects in the complex and vast universe. I am also amazed by the ease in applying the diagrams; even amateurs can deduce one or two of them, which is a testament to the perfect fusion of generality, applicability, experimentalism and commonality. Then, when can we develop a comparable schema for the accounting profession that can cover the past, present and future, and risks and opportunities of enterprises, and increase the confidence of members of the accounting profession and dissipate the doubts of outsiders?

In *On Capital*, Karl Marx first performed a scientific abstraction by abstracting tens of millions of enterprises with different production conditions in different sectors into enterprises with medium-level production conditions; industrial, commercial, financial and land capitalists into a "general" capitalist; and complex labor into simple labor. He also abstracted the absoluteness of commodity value and researched the rules of residual value in terms of the relativity of commodity value. Marx then went from abstraction to concretization and applied the conclusions from scientific abstraction to analyze specific problems and draw universal conclusions. Such an abstract way of thinking is of great importance for academic research, policy-making and practical work today.

Studying the classics in mathematics and natural sciences can also help us develop a scientific way of thinking. Lu Yongxiang, vice chairman of the Standing Committee of the National People's Congress, once stated that mathematics is not a natural science but the science of thinking. The holistic, abstract and logical ways of thinking and the methods of induction and deduction in mathematics can help us perform deep scientific thinking. In the history of mathematics, China is credited with making many groundbreaking contributions. For example, *Nine-Chapter Arithmetic* and Zu Chongzhi's accurate calculation of the circumferential ratio have had a lasting influence on human civilization and thinking. Another good case is the book *Harmonic Analysis of Multiple Complex Variables in Typical Domains* by the accomplished modern mathematician Hua Luogeng. The precise analytical methods and research findings used by Hua have far-reaching implications for the study of harmonic analysis, complex analysis, and differential equation; they have also been widely praised for the methodology employed, winning extensive admiration in China and beyond. In particular, the highly popular "optimum seeking method"[4] has exerted a significant influence on our socioeconomic life.

It should be noted that mathematics and mathematical thinking have always exerted a significant influence on accounting and accounting thinking. Research by Professor Guo Daoyang and other scholars has shown that in the initial stages of human society, accounting behavior occurred and evolved simultaneously with primitive mathematical behavior.

The formation of the bookkeeping theory, in particular, was deeply influenced by mathematical thinking. In 1494, Italian mathematician and accounting scholar Luca Pacioli published his book entitled *Everything about Arithmetic, Geometry, and Proportions* (also known as *Mathematical Formulation and Generalization*). The "bookkeeping theory" in the book contained the first formula for debit-credit bookkeeping, which was built according to mathematical principles and the debit-credit balance principle. The book illustrated the theory of invariable debit-credit balance. These theories were subsequently adopted by accounting scholars as basic principles and became the fundamental rules for auditing accounts and reviewing statements. Accounting historians argue that it was not until the publication of Pacioli's book that accounting was separated from accounting practice, began to develop its own theoretical research and eventually grew into an academic discipline.

Today, mathematical thinking exerts an even more profound influence on accounting theory and practice. In the face of increasingly complicated economic affairs and frequent economic transactions, it is essential to apply the holistic, abstract and logical thinking in mathematics to gain an insight into the nature of affairs and transactions before proper accounting treatment can be performed. Moreover, if new breakthroughs are to be made in the study of accounting theory and a firm footing is to be secured at the forefront of world accounting theory, it is vital to apply a solid empirical research methodology. This is not possible without the application of mathematical thinking and methodology.

The same holds true for other natural sciences. We may say that each classical work on natural science is a classical work on scientific thinking. By reading, appreciating, researching and understanding classical works, our way of thinking will be constantly integrated and enriched and become more scientific. It will also help us to convert the wisdom of the sages into contemporary thinking power, guiding us to strive for greater prosperity for the accounting profession.

- **Grasping the truth:** Studying classics can be a shortcut to exploring and discovering the nature of things and patterns of change. Studying classics will allow us to experience the delights of "ascending the mountain's crest which dwarfs all peaks under my feet."[5] Studying classics will help us to experience the thrill of unraveling the mysteries of heaven and earth, the changes from ancient to modern times and the numerous schools of thought. It can help us to appreciate the authors' expression of truth and their exploration of human nature, which will enable us to tell right from wrong, separate truth from falsehood, gain an insight into the future, and enlighten our minds. Classics are a link between past and future, a bridge between society and nature, and a mirror of humanity and morality. By studying them, we can acquire a rapid understanding of the nature and meaning of the development of things, society and humankind. This is true for all classical works on humanities, history, science and technology, ancient or modern, Chinese or foreign.

The Book of Changes, for example, stated, "If I have fine wine, I will share it with my friends, and we will enjoy the wine under the rising wind and scudding clouds." This points us to the important principle of ensuring that all people share the fruits of the nation's reform and opening-up. The egalitarian thoughts expressed in *Laozi* ("to take away from those that have too much and give to those that have not enough") and the thinking on consumer ethics set out in *Guanzi* enable us to have a better understanding of the sound consumption theory that emphasizes restraining desires in life and reasonably restraining consumer behavior. The statement in *The Art of War* that "what is of supreme importance in war is to attack the enemy's strategy; next best is to disrupt his alliances by diplomacy; the next best is to attack his army; and the worst policy is to attack cities" allows us to recognize the principle that "to subdue the enemy without fighting is the supreme excellence." By reading Sima Qian's *Historical Records*, we can find out about the acts of numerous historical figures, understand and discover how state regimes operated, the status and role of individuals in the regime, and the constraints and contradictions that institutions faced.

In his *Critique of Practical Reason*, Immanuel Kant stated, "Two things fill the mind with ever new and increasing admiration and awe as well as piety and belief, the more often and steadily we reflect upon them: The starry heavens above me and the moral law within me." This statement gives us a feel of the philosopher's painstaking exploration and deep contemplation of practical realities and future prospects. After reading this work, I reflected upon my late teacher Yang Shizhan's educational career, writings and personal life and pondered the new requirements and challenges facing the accounting profession today. I managed to lift myself out of a messy dilemma and straighten my thoughts; eventually, I was able to capture my observations and feelings in my article *Looking Up*, winning positive comments from relevant parties.

Reading *On the Revolutions of the Heavenly Spheres* by Nicolaus Copernicus, we came to recognize that the earth is not the center of the universe, but just one of the planets, and we gained a deep understanding of this fundamental revolution in astronomy and a solid feel of how the revolution eventually led to the emergence of modern astronomy and ushered in a fresh era for the advancement of natural science. Reading *The Origin of Species* by Charles Darwin, we came to recognize that "all variations in the organic world and the inorganic world occur as a result of the laws of nature rather than the invention of gods." Lenin stated, "Darwin's work finally drove God away from nature, allowing biological science to rise."

Reading *The Selected Works of Deng Xiaoping*, we grasp Deng's scientific assertion regarding the nature of socialism, the fundamental line of "one central point and two basic points," the basic fulfillment of the strategic task of modernization "in three steps", and the fundamental guideline of giving "equal importance to economic development on one hand and to the development of socialist culture and ideology on the other hand."

In short, we advocate studying classics so that we can establish proper values and build a noble and independent character, enlighten our minds, and improve our intelligence and our capacity to understand, thereby developing our ability to identify and resolve problems in a more rational and scientific manner. Studying classics will also train our thinking so that we can reflect on our life and explore the rules of change and development in socioeconomic life and mother nature over a longer period of time, in a vaster space, and at a higher level. Moreover, studying classics will help us to grasp the truth so that we can build on the legacy they have given us in accordance with the needs and developments of a new era.

Only those who take pleasure in and are good at studying the classics are able to absorb nutrients from them and to mature and progress constantly. The same is true for a profession and a team. Only by constantly absorbing nutrients and extracting the essence of what is good from the past can we avoid becoming conservative or complacent and can we strengthen and expand our undertakings.

Following 30 years of reform and opening-up, the accountancy profession is presently at a major historical juncture in which it takes a greater leap, exerts a greater influence, and pursues excellence. The environment in which we live, the situation we are facing, and the tasks we are to fulfill are undergoing profound change. The requirements on accounting professionals are becoming increasingly stringent. Thus, it has never been more important and urgent to study classics. You are the outstanding members of today's accounting profession and its future inheritors; on you falls the task of renewing the vigor and standing of the profession. A single word may provoke the thoughts of millions and may change the destinies of many. Make friends with the classics and learn how to manage your careers and your lives in the process. To delay one more day, is to endure one more day of mediocrity. I hope that all of us will make the best use of these golden years and let the vastness and profoundness of the classics shine as a beacon on our life journey, guiding us to greater development for accounting reform and development in the new era.

HOW TO STUDY CLASSICS

Dongfang Shuo of the Han Dynasty once claimed: "I've studied literature and history for three years and I think my knowledge in these subjects is sufficient." Du Fu of the Tang Dynasty announced: "I've read more than 10,000 scrolls of books." After that, however, the increasing application of movable-type printing produced too many books for any one person to read. Given the even greater pressures facing people today in this regard, we need to find a practical response to the question: How should we study the vast range of classics which provide specialist knowledge in different fields?

Wang Yunwu, a renowned modern educator, who was hailed by *New York Times* as "a cultural messenger in the 1930s who brought books rather than bullets to China in hardship," summed up 14 steps to study: Set goals, do the groundwork, select a topic, progress steadily, get a general idea of the book, draw an outline, resolve doubts, compare, be dedicated, use references, work hard, persevere, identify the key points of the book, and refresh the memory from time to time. Wang also suggested reading light books at leisure, reading classic books intensively, skimming voluminous books, and reading the digests of certain books. I think this suggestion is very useful and I'd like to add a few observations of my own, based on my personal reading experience.

Read thoroughly and review constantly the books in which you are interested: Interest is the foundation for studying classics. British writer Somerset Maugham proposed "reading for pleasure." Elaborating on this, he said:

> No matter how scholars comment on a book, even though they unanimously lavish praise on it, if it fails to arouse your interest, for you, it remains not useful at all. Remember that even critics make mistakes. Many blunders in the history of criticism were made by celebrated critics. You are the best judge of the significance of the book you are reading for yourself.

In other words, follow your feelings, as this is the most pleasant way to read classics, just like drinking water to quench thirst, eating to fill an empty stomach, and taking medicine to cure a disease. Zhu Xiaoyuan, a professor of history at Peking University, said:

> . . . people do not want to know about things totally familiar to them and fail to understand things completely unfamiliar to them as a result of a distance too far. What people most want to know is things familiar yet unfamiliar . . . At that point, people enter a good condition and if they devote their heart and soul, they will be able to draw upon the essence of books.

Intuitively, like Zhu, they will figure out "what love is and what is needed" and experience "the most intriguing aroma of life and the dense flavor of its heaviest fruit."

Thorough reading and constant review are important methods for studying classics. It is the same with tasting oolong tea—the real taste does not come out until the second or third brewing. Even people with exceptionally sharp powers of observation should try to imagine themselves as an empty cup waiting to sample the tea, opening themselves up and allowing the books to flow into the heart. At different times, in different places, in different capacities, with different experiences and with different mindsets, a reader may get different insights and experiences from the same book. I wonder if you have ever experienced that feeling that can come when you re-read a book that you read in childhood and suddenly what once seemed abstruse and hard to understand now appears simple and clear? Or, what may have seemed insignificant years ago turns out to be important now? Reviewing classical works constantly can lead you to new discoveries.

In an article entitled "The Five Books that Have Influenced Me for 20 Years," which appeared in the *Finance and Accounting* journal earlier this year, Wang Lun talked about ways of reading books, and I find them very enlightening. At one point he spoke of his experience of reading *Philosophy and the Contemporary World* for the second time:

> I read in a communicative manner. I sent the book by post to an overseas friend, and she also sent me a related book. Later, before the books were sent back, we both wrote a lot of our viewpoints in the notes; our views might be similar or different. When I read the book for the third time, my notes had grown to more than 20,000 words, largely as a result of our exchange of ideas.

I am not saying that we must do the same, but this is definitely a good way to read a book thoroughly and to review it constantly.

Studying classics on topics that appeal to you will give you a lot of pleasure and can take your thinking to new levels. *Historical Records* relates an episode in which Confucius was discussing music with a minister of the State of Qi. So intrigued was he by Shao tunes that he studied Shao music for three months, "during which he was so engrossed that he found meat tasteless." In *The Legend of Gentleman Wu Liu*, Tao Yuanming said that whenever he was engrossed in a book he would gladly forget about his meals. It should be noted, however, that to achieve this state Tao Yuanming had "to be in peace and quiet without consideration of glory or money." It is clear then that to get the most out of the classics the reader should approach them with genuine curiosity and enthusiasm. They should command his undivided attention, with all mundane concerns set aside so that the book and the reader can become one. Conversely, if the reader is agitated, eager to voice opinions on everything, chases fame and profit, and ostentatiously pretends that he has total understanding of the classics and has truth in his hand, he will never be able to attain such a level.

For you people attending this workshop, this process will not be a problem, as all of you have had the pleasant experience of opening a new book and learning something useful. The fact that you are here shows that you have an interest in books, and read regularly. But interest levels can fluctuate and disappear like a puff of smoke if we do not maintain the practice of reading continuously. This requires that you foster a conscious interest. This can be time-consuming and will test your willpower. But there is a clear aim to this: To progress from a simple quest for knowledge to conscientious in-depth contemplation of whether the theories presented in the classics hold water, whether the data cited are accurate, and whether the conclusions are applicable to reality. This involves making an effort to dig deeper.

There is a considerable difference between "liking" the classics and "enjoying" them. The former indicates being enthusiastic about studying and keen to explore what they have to say. Enjoyment, on the other hand, only comes to those who have made studying classics part of their lives and thus deepened their understanding through the process of lengthy exploration. They are infatuated with the classics and their interest is a subconscious one. They display a strong will and delight in the thrill of pursuit. Classics will be a permanent presence on your desks, your "talisman." After going through the three stages of knowing, liking and enjoying, the interest in studying classics will take root in our hearts and play an instrumental role in our pursuits within the accounting profession.

Usain Bolt, the Jamaican sprinter who won gold medals in the 100– and 200–meter events at the 2008 Summer Olympics in Beijing, breaking the Olympic and world records in the process, has been dubbed "the fastest man on earth." When asked about the secret of his success, this bubbly young man blurted out, "I love sprinting; I love sports!" I think our leading accounting talents can learn something from Bolt's unbridled passion. Let "I study classics, therefore I am!" be our motto. Let's allow classics to turn the noise around us into soothing light music.

Be goal-driven: Normally, people study classics out of curiosity, but this is not enough for you leading talents in accounting; you should study them for a good reason, and the good reason is your great ambitions. You should be driven by your goals. Karl Marx devoted almost his entire life to writing his monumental work *On Capital*, calling upon all oppressed people around the world to throw off their shackles and win freedom and happiness. Marx read practically all the classical works on philosophy, political economics and sociology available in his time. It took him 24 years from collecting materials to completing the first draft.

Pu Songling, author of *Liao Zhai Zhi Yi* (*Strange Stories from a Chinese Studio*), was never successful in imperial examinations, but he did not turn bitter; rather, he found inspiration in the story of the Xiang Yu, who ordered his troops to break their cooking pots and sink their boats to drive home the message that there was no way for them to retreat and that the only way they could survive was to advance and keep fighting. He also drew inspiration from the story of Gou Jian, the King of Yue, who endured self-imposed hardship by sleeping on brushwood and tasting galls, to strengthen his resolve to realize his ambition. Pu wrote: "Where there is a will, there is a way . . . Heaven never fails people with steely willpower."

Pu took this as his motto. I think that if we added two lines from Tang-Dynasty poet Wang Bo's *Preface to Tengwang Tower*—"With old age comes greater strengths and determination; how can people start thinking about changing their ambitions in old age? Poverty toughens character and helps sustain lofty aspirations"—Pu's motto would be complete. The resilient Pu eventually became a classical figure with his collection of short stories, putting himself on a par in both literary accomplishment and influence with the most successful candidates in the imperial examinations.

In the face of today's opportunities and challenges, leading talents in accounting should aim higher, and draw inspiration from the ancient proverb that "as heaven maintains vigor through movements, a gentleman should constantly strive for self-perfection." They should also try to gain a deep understanding of the real meaning of the saying "Goals must be set like mountains in order to be firm; roads should be walked as if in water in order to reach the destination in spite of the twists and turns." They should aim as high as possible and strive to fulfill the mission they are charged with. Under the guidance of their lofty ambitions, they can make studying classics a habit, a spiritual pursuit, and an indispensable part of their lives. Let classics drill our thinking, enhance our thinking capacity, and boost our creative capacity, so that we can constantly improve and enrich ourselves, boost careers, and make our lives more exciting.

Be persevering, diligent and energetic: In striving to achieve our goals we must read extensively in order to think extensively, read intensively in order to gain enlightenment, and persevere in order to attain the essence. Mao Zedong was an avid reader throughout his lifetime; he read extensively in literature, art, military history, philosophy and sociology. Whether on horseback during the years of war or bedridden in his twilight years, Mao always had the classics as company. The margins of his copy of *The 24 Histories* were filled with his handwritten comments and annotations, which were incisive, insightful and thought-provoking, reflecting his deep thinking and profound understanding. In the days when cataracts impaired his vision, he adopted the "reading by ear" method created by Yang Dayan in ancient times and instructed his staff to read literary works to him. Throughout his life, he practiced what he advocated in a couplet that he had written in his early years, the gist of which is: If you study diligently and persistently you can learn a lot without having to get up early and stay up late; and you'll learn nothing if you study for one day and then rest for the next 10 days. Mao set a very good example for us in studying classics and Xun Zi's words remind us of the benefits of perseverance, "Rain and wind will arise where soil gathers to form a high mountain; the dragon will emerge where water accumulated to form a deep pond." We, too, should adopt this kind of perseverance.

Li Dazhao[6] spoke of those among us who think that the time we save is for relaxation only. For him, "The more time saved, the more time can be devoted to reading. Reading and working do not interfere with each other; rather, it's real life to combine working and reading." In this regard, renowned writer Li Guowen is a role model. He has extensive interests in all fields of literature and is highly accomplished, having won all major awards for contemporary Chinese literature. He has also distinguished himself as a leading historical prose writer. One critic described him as "one of the best contemporary prose writers in integrating knowledge, personality and observation, reminiscent of the style of French writer Montaigne." Behind Li's success lies painstaking research. When writing about a certain historical figure, he didn't merely repeat what had been said already. Rather, he made a study of all related literature to establish the facts.

Li's approach is also applicable to the study of classics in other fields. For example, to understand Samuelson's *Economics* (dubbed "the greatest economics textbook of all time") the reader needs to be patient, diligent and persevering, and deep-thinking. During the reading process, sometimes it may be necessary to refer to the works of past or present economics gurus and think deeply. Sometimes, it may be necessary to make comparisons and conduct analyses in light of current socioeconomic phenomena in order to deepen understanding. At other times, it may be important to perform complex mathematical calculations which, though shunned by many, may be the only way to gain a proper understanding of monumental books such as *Economics*. To take another example: To gain a deep understanding of Eldon S. Hendriksen's *Accounting Theory*, the reader must also possess a fairly high level of accounting knowledge and the reading process will be a "painstaking" experience.

"Keeping silently in mind what has been read, studying hard and feeling contented, and teaching others tirelessly" were three tasks that Confucius regularly performed. Here, "silently" does not just mean a way of reading; more importantly, it requires us to devote ourselves, heart and soul, to studies. Paul Dirac, the renowned physicist who created the complete theoretical formulation of quantum mechanics, was pondering even when he was taking a walk. Throughout history, famous personages noted in China and elsewhere for their wisdom were all good examples of "keeping silently in mind what has been read." This process will help us get into the habit of studying anytime, anywhere, and applying observations and insights from the classics to current realities. Only in this way can we truly absorb the essence of the classics, improve our qualifications and knowledge, and elevate the purpose of our life.

A mesh must consist of longitudinal and latitudinal threads. After building a solid foundation of "addition", we may progress to "multiplication" and achieve a substantial breakthrough. Only with great effort can we make the transition from quantitative improvement to qualitative improvement, to figure out the "way" hidden in the classics and experience the excitement akin to that of the poet in the line: "When all at once I turn my head, she is there where lantern light is dimly shed."[7]

Feel it with your mind: Once you open a classical work, you are transported from the commonplace into a deep time when you can have a unique conversation with the noble souls enshrined there. In this concealed deep time, we can consult with the creators of the classics, experience the feelings they once enjoyed, and feel their thoughts in an exchange of views that span generations, trades and oceans. In this way, our thinking will be nourished and elevated to a higher level. Zhu Xiaoyuan, a professor of history at Peking University said: "If you read books with your body, you will get knowledge; if you read books with your brain, you will get rationality; and if you read books with your mind, you will get feelings and insights." In the process of interacting with the classics, the reader changes, and understands himself more fully and moves towards that self. Sir John Lubbock of Britain said: "Books guide us through adversity, soothe our minds, and help us shake off the shackle of sorrow and pain; books turn otherwise dull and boring times into pleasant days;

books fill our brains with various beliefs so that our brains are full of noble and joyful thoughts; as a result, we lose ourselves in the books and lift our soul."

Celebrated Chinese writer Ba Jin once reminisced about how he read an abridged translation of the book *To the Young People,* written by renowned Russian revolutionary and geologist Pyotr Nikolaevich Kropotkin. Ba said: "I never expected such a book in the world! It's full of remarks that I wanted to say but failed to express clearly. It's very clear, rational and eloquent, and its inflammatory style of writing can burn the heart of a 15-year-old child to ashes." *To the Young People* and many other classic works, such as Polish writer Leopold Kampf's *Am Vorabend*, opened the young Ba Jin's eyes to the world, prompting him to reflect upon himself and triggering in him a strong consciousness of how to think and act. As a result, he threw himself into the movement against dictatorship and power and embarked upon a pursuit of independence and liberty.

While such experiences may not be as powerful or as dramatic in our adult lives, studying classics as a way of exploring the possibilities of self has far greater implications for achieving qualitative self-improvements, expanding capacity, and illuminating the path forward than for the young. Hence, in addition to fostering a keen interest and being goal-driven and diligent, the reader is also expected to experience and feel with the mind.

For example, China's calligraphic art, especially the cursive hand, such as the wild cursive hand of the Tang Dynasty's Zhang Xu and Huai Su and that of the great statesman Mao Zedong, can be hard to understand and appreciate through rational analysis, which just makes us more confused. Likewise, we can never rationally figure out the expression of emotions of the Olympic gold medalists who instantly kneel down or lie down at the moment of victory. We can just use our senses and minds to embrace and experience the power of their bearing and the beauty of youth, power, freedom and transcendence.

In Zen Buddhism, the mind can only be at perfect peace when it is free from craving, anger and other afflictive states. But this is not something that can be transmitted from one person to another through words. Enlightenment can only come through meditation and direct experience, rather than from acquiring purely theoretical knowledge.

To understand the classics with the mind, it's vital to experience their "taste." According to *Dream Pool Essays* by Shen Kuo, "In ancient times, it was common for people to use strong-scented herbs to keep worms away from their books." This is perhaps the origin of the Chinese term for "book aroma." While the aroma and taste to which I'm referring here are not literal in this way, they may nevertheless be sour, sweet, bitter or spicy according to the senses of the individual reader. Viewpoints in the classics may not necessarily be what we've expected or in line with current realities. The thoughts they express may be unappealing or not readily comprehensible and may require great effort to figure them out. Yet, more often than not, it is the wisdom contained in the classics that provides guidance for us and enables us to experience the thrill of enlightenment. All these are the "tastes" in the classics which can be sampled, and this sampling always leaves people with pleasant feelings. The pleasure to be gained from appreciating the classics is endless. "The ultimate realm of humans and books is to transcend reading"[8]—even more so when it comes to classic works.

There is a precondition to comprehending the classics with the mind—the reader must have accumulated knowledge, thought and experience. In his book *Wenxin Diaolong: Shensi* (*The Literary Heart and the Carving of Dragons: Magic Thinking*), Liu Xie said that the ability to have "embarked on deep contemplation on subjects that span a thousand years and to be touched as if one could see the vistas one thousand kilometers away" is built upon "an accumulation of knowledge and constant reflection upon life." Although confined to a wheelchair, Stephen Hawking, renowned British scientist and author of *A Brief History of Time*, is able to cruise the boundless universe through his mind, with his vast knowledge as the vehicle. Huang Binhong, an eminent Chinese painter, drew his inspiration from his unique understanding of ancient people and Mother Nature. Before the age of 50, he studied numerous schools of painting in the Tang and Song dynasties. In his fifties and sixties, he ascended the Yellow Mountain nine times, Jiuhua Mountain five times, Tai Mountain four times, scaled the Five Ridges and Yandang Mountain, and traveled the length and breadth of Sichuan. He drew upon the strengths of many eminent painters of the past, improved his painting skills by copying the works of leading painters, and drew inspiration from natural landscapes, eventually becoming a leading painter in his seventies. In his twilight years, he summarized Chinese painting techniques as "five strokes" (smooth, slick, round, duplicated, and changeable) and "seven inks" (thick, light, splashing, soaking, accumulated, focused, and sticky ink), which later became classic techniques among his followers and contributed significantly to the development of the elegant style of Chinese painting.

Understanding classics with our minds allows our souls to communicate with the souls of the classics and to gain the motivation as well as to absorb nutrients for growth and development. Let classics become the guidelines in shaping our character and steering us to greater career prosperity.

Make use of criticism to gain a better understanding: The classics illuminate the past, present and future, guiding our spirits to travel beyond the horizon towards a farther destination, and filling us with a sense of the sacred and awe for life. Yet neither they nor their creators can be detached from the era and environment from which they arose. That is, they tend to bear the marks of a specific era. While we should be respectful and humble towards classics, they are not be swallowed whole; rather, they should be chewed and digested. This is not to negate classics; it's a genuine form of respect for them. Readers should not be restricted by the classics or be passive recipients. Rather, they should be confident that they will contribute to the development of the classics.

Classics achieve that status precisely because they interact with readers, who inject fresh vitality into them, add new dimensions to them, and shed new light on them. We may say that the historic evolution of classics is a process of gradual outward expansion of concentric circles in line with new developments.

Thus, the ultimate achievement in studying classics is to transcend them and their creators, to read them in a vaster space, to judge them from a post-development perspective. If these conditions are met, the reader will marvel at Adam Smith's *The Wealth of Nations* and at his emergence as the undisputed founding father of modern economics through smashing the mercantile doctrine and advocating new thinking on free competition and market economy. At the same time, the reader may also feel regret about the Great Depression, which arose from the failure of the "invisible hand" as a market mechanism. Moreover, the reader may find there the basis of the emergence of Keynesianism and the US government's *Emergency Economic Stabilization Act* of 2008.

For another example, while readers of *Li Sao* may be struck by the author Qu Yuan's extraordinary patriotism, his uprightness and his disregard for personal interest, they may also regret that he did not seek a balance between knowing when to advance and when to retreat in the political fights.[9]

I believe that readers must be bold. In the words of Mencius: "Accepting what a book says without reservation is worse than having no book in the first place." It's important to raise questions, establish topics and have a strong awareness of problems so that the mind can stay in an active state of research. Lin Yutang hit the nail right on the head by saying that "boldness, a sharp eye and willpower are required when reading a book. The ultimate purpose of reading a book is to enliven the mind. Boldness means that the reader must have opinions, even though they may differ from their predecessors' views." It's also important to avoid falling into a rut and becoming pedantic, which may "turn your brain into the racecourse of our predecessors' thoughts" as Schopenhauer put it.

It's important to have a bold vision when studying and appreciating classics. Celebrated Tang Dynasty historian Liu Zhiji is a good case in point. He was noted for his tendency to question past philosophers and to elaborate on the errors of predecessors. He wrote:

> I have been an avid reader since my childhood and I'm fond of talking about famous principles. My findings are all the result of strenuous thinking rather than hearsay. In my childhood, I read *The Book of the Han Dynasty* by Ban Gu and *The Book of the Post-Han Period* by Xie Cheng, and I thought that *The List of Past and Present Personages* should not have occurred in *The Book of the Han Dynasty*, and that *The Book of the Post-Han Period* should have begun with Emperor Liu Xuan. I raised these questions but the adults ridiculed me, claiming that I was a kid who knew nothing and that past sages were not to be questioned. I felt ashamed, thinking that I must have been wrong, and had no more to say. However, when I read through the collections of essays by Zhang Heng and Fan Ye, my suspicion that *The Book of the Han Dynasty* and *The Book of the Post-Han Period* must be wrong was confirmed.

Liu's boldness in raising questions based on his own understanding, rather than simply following established theories, eventually enabled him to produce China's first history criticism book, *Shi Tong*, earning him the admiration of future generations.

Similar cases abound in the financial accounting field. For example, classic works on capital structure and asset pricing in modern financial theories have led to six Nobel laureates in economics. New findings are always achieved on the sound basis of our critical inheritance, of working within existing knowledge structures, questioning them and making substantive breakthroughs from bold hypotheses. If we never make an effort to criticize or surpass them, the classics will become rigid and lose their appeal and our academic research will stagnate.

We should start with details such as the annotations and indexes in the classics, which often tell us the origins and basis of the conclusions they reach. Here, we may encounter contentions between different views and what lay behind them. We may see how these different perspectives, methods of evaluation and critiques were absorbed to refine or improve the classics. Once we have a grasp of this information, we will be well grounded to evaluate the classics.

If we start from the details, our evaluation can be expanded to include how the ideas held by classic figures influenced the economy and society at the time and how they have been assessed since. For instance, when criticizing the work of the renowned American economist and 1976 Nobel Laureate Milton Friedman, it is not enough to simply focus on books such as *A Monetary History of the United States* (co-authored with Anna Schwartz), *Capitalism and Freedom*, and *Price Theory*. When we look into why he was awarded the Nobel Prize for his theory of consumption function, monetary history and market stabilization policy, why his monetary theory was adopted by three American presidents (Richard Nixon, Henry Ford and Ronald Reagan—even George W. Bush acknowledged him as a revolutionary thinker and an outstanding economist whose work has furthered human dignity and freedom), we might also consider some other questions: Why is it that certain British scholars claimed that there were limitations in Friedman's academic thinking and theoretical system, limitations that resulted in at least three million people in Britain losing their jobs? Why was Friedman opposed to European economic integration on the grounds that the national borders and different cultures in Europe would make it difficult to implement a single currency and that the introduction of the euro would create economic shockwaves and political conflict? (Despite this, the euro was introduced as planned and without the predicted consequences.) Once we have asked such questions, we will be in the position to give a more comprehensive, objective and fair judgment of Friedman's work. Our comprehension of his theories and thoughts will reach a new level in the process.

The emphasis on comparative study should also encompass comparison with similar works. For example, our judgment on Keynes, the British economist, should not be limited to *The General Theory of Employment, Interest and Money,* which constitutes the theoretical framework of macroeconomic management. It should also be linked back to the works of Adam Smith and Karl Marx, and forward to Friedman. Through such integration and comparison, we are able to understand the necessity of Keynes' assertion that "the government has to intervene in the operation of the macro economy," and identify some of the limitations that this important, era-marked, economic idea exhibits. Based on this, we may evaluate the contributions of the economic masters. From the clashes between these ideas, through which views are discredited and established, we may comprehend more fully the prominent role of economics in social sciences as we see it today.

As this script was being revised, the US Government announced that it would take over two mortgage giants—Fannie Mae (Federal National Mortgage Association) and Freddie Mac (Federal Home Loan Mortgage Corporation)—and the *Emergency Economic Stabilization Act* was eventually adopted after considerable debate. There was a mix of praise and censure for this move, which went against the spirit of a free-market economy, and opinions were widely divided. But this decision, based on painstaking and complex thinking, has led us into a new, more profound domain of economics.

The information contained in the classics has to be extracted, linked and integrated into current realities. Only when contemporary information is used to verify and examine the classics can "all history be read as contemporary history."[10]

Zhu Xi, the Song Dynasty philosopher, educator and a great master of neo-Confucianism tells us:

> To read characters, give faith to the original sentence and do not willingly add new characters; if there are any cracks, they should be exposed naturally, like a box, and not forced; also, one should not read with a pre-established doctrine, and use the meanings of the ancients to serve a doctrine.

Our comprehension of the classics would reach a new level if we were adept at identifying inadequacies ("cracks") therein that are in conflict with common sense, and then making down-to-earth critiques.

WHAT CLASSICS ARE TO BE STUDIED
AND APPRECIATED?

The history of human civilization is also a history of how the classics came to be. Given the limitations of time, energy and the scope of our knowledge, it is both impossible and unnecessary for us to read all of the classics. A careful selection is thus required if we are to avoid the harm that can come from mere passive acceptance without testing them against our own understanding.

In the field of accounting, we should value structure and quality, as opposed to quantity. In consultation with a number of chief accountants, senior partners in accounting firms, accounting professors and government officials, I came up with a list of the essential classics, which are roughly divided into five categories:

- Politics and Natural Sciences
- Humanities
- Economics
- Management
- Accounting and Auditing.[11]

It should be pointed out that this is merely a rough classification, and is by no means exhaustive. There may be a certain degree of overlapping between the categories. It is recommended that each person makes further adjustments and selections in line with their own circumstances.

Here, I would like to discuss some views from which we all may draw encouragement.

Firstly, fields are to be broadened. Attention should also be given to classic texts in other categories, something which is not widely practiced at present. Some of these are of great significance and can help us towards a further understanding of the classic texts within our own specialist field. They are what we might call "the stones from other hills [that] may be used to polish gems." A blind partiality for confining our reading to the standard texts of our own specialty is very likely to do us harm, just as forest ecosystems with only a single species of tree often experience a drastic drop in biodiversity, soil fertility and water conservation, leaving them prone to fire, diseases and pests. In fact, some people have become learned masters in their own area of specialty because they draw from other sources. Take the economist Friedrich von Hayek, for instance. In his seminal work, *The Constitution of Liberty*, he spends the whole of Volume One discussing the philosophical question "What is freedom?" It is on this fertile ground that he then goes on to expound his liberal economic theories in Volume Two.

Here, I would like to stress the importance of the humanities. Whether we look at historical and philosophical masterpieces or unrivalled works of literature, they are inevitably grounded in human nature and oriented towards human well-being and harmony. They convey the unchanging essence of the human spirit and the values they possess are timeless. According to *The Book of Changes*, "Humanity is found in civilization. Guided by astronomy, one can detect the changes of time; guided by humanity, one can be civilized". Classic texts in the humanities can show us the true meaning of freedom and wisdom. They can guide us as we ponder the purpose, meaning and value of life, and thus establish an ideal personality and goal, for which we are willing to fight throughout our lives.

There is indeed a need for us to read and reflect on these classics. The great figures of the European Renaissance are all models in this regard. "That was a time that gave birth to giants," Engels said, and these giants were all multi-talented, knowledgeable people.

There is a rhetorical device in literature known as "synesthesia;" which refers to a break from the boundaries of vision, hearing, smell, taste and touch, and allows each of the senses to communicate with one another so as to depict feelings towards objective things. In his *Moonlight in the Lotus Pond*, for example, Zhu Ziqing depicted the "breaths of fragrance" from the lotuses as being "just like a faint sound of singing drifting from a distant building." The masters in the Renaissance, who may be rightly called "universal geniuses," had this ability to bring together several spheres of experience to create a newer, fuller meaning in concrete form. They broke the constraints of categories and achieved outstanding accomplishments in a multiplicity of fields, each reinforcing and furthering the other. As Engels put it, "They did not become slaves of the division of labor." Indeed, Leonardo da Vinci not only mastered four or five foreign languages, but was also highly accomplished in art, architecture, engineering, philosophy, music and mathematics.

Much the same could be said about the May Fourth Period, known as the "Chinese Renaissance." Most of those in China's first, second and third generations of natural scientists recorded marvelous achievements in other fields in addition to their significant accomplishments in their own discipline.

Imagine what it would be like if an individual lacked basic humanity. Pan Guangdan, who was one of the most distinguished sociologists and eugenicists as well a renowned expert in education in the Republic of China period, offered us a good metaphor: Science is like a knife; if those who have mastered scientific knowledge are deprived of humanity, the possible prospect may be "like a child wielding a sword; a great many injuries would occur." Expanding on this for accountants, if we cannot establish the human spirit of integrity as the characteristic of our era, the more proficient our accounting techniques are, the more severe the negative effects from forgery and fraud will be. In this sense, while stressing the reading of classics in finance, accounting and auditing, accountants should also pay special attention to the study of classics in the humanities. This is so that we can cultivate a spirit of moral integrity.

Secondly, the classic texts should be carefully selected. Zheng Banqiao, one of Eight Outstanding Painters in Yangzhou during the Qing Dynasty, once remarked: "It is highly rewarding to pursue quality instead of quantity while reading; only a well-digested read can be of use, while excessive reading is simply fruitless." To Francis Bacon, "Some books are to be tasted, others to be swallowed, and some few to be chewed and digested." The focus of our study should be on the "stars" among the classics. After these core works have been thoroughly read and well digested, our study will become easier and easier.

For example, in order to understand Western culture, reading *The Bible* is a must. It is the basis upon which many other classic works in Western religion and philosophy are grounded. Likewise, it would be impossible to gain an understanding of twentieth-century China without first understanding the works of Lu Xun. It should be noted that to read and study the "core" classics, one must read the original versions, and not various interpretations. Regarding this, Engels gave an incisive exposition. In a letter to a friend on the topic of how to approach study, Engels wrote in August 1884:

> Study should begin with the true classics, and not from the simplified versions of those least desired books on German economics or the scripts from the authors of these materials . . . most importantly, we

must conscientiously study classical economics, from the physio-
cratic school to Smith, Ricardo and their schools. Also, we have to
study the works of Saint-Simon, Fourier and Owen and those of
Marx; at the same time, we should make continuous efforts to draw
our own views.

In other words, it is necessary for us to read original works
systematically. As Engels put it: "[B]y studying the originals ourselves,
we will not be led astray by simplified and other second-hand
materials."

Thirdly, we must plan. People have different needs, sentiments and
capabilities at different stages of life. What we read should be determined by circumstance—whether we are studying in school, doing
academic research, working in specific operations, assuming a particular leadership role, and so on. For example, while in school, the
ability to comprehend is still developing and growing. However, this is
the period where the mind is active and we are full of energy; and so it
is advisable to read broadly without having to rush for the pursuit of
mastery. At the academic research stage, one is advised to focus on the
established academic direction, reading widely and in-depth from the
body of classical texts related to the profession as a foundation for
further studies into other classics outside the profession.

With the gradual accumulation of life experience, the classics read
at a young age have to be re-read and meditated upon later in life,
when new insights will surely arise. Some classics are best read during
adulthood, such as the hundreds of academic materials compiled in the
Book of Changes. Confucius' saying, "Learning the Book of Changes
is easy at 50" is a nugget of truth. Of course, this is not to say that it can
only be understood at that precise age. As modern society progresses
and people are more exposed to the world through education, the ideal
time for learning can be brought forward.

Fourthly, we must read for ourselves. To obtain the full flavor of
the classics, it is necessary to read the original works as they were
written. Not to do so runs the risk of accepting somebody else's
potentially superficial interpretation, such as often occurs when classic
texts are adapted for a television audience. As leading accounting
talents, we must embrace the texts to obtain direct nourishment from
them. We must form our own list of such books, professional and non-
professional, and cultivate the habit of reading so that it becomes an
integral part of our lives.

As I mentioned earlier, in addition to the established classic texts, there is a vast array of other human experience that perhaps lies beyond words and yet can be invaluable in shaping that experience and the way forward. They may be "read" or "tasted" while visiting an ancient site, admiring a picture, watching an epic film or simply by being in a particular place at a particular time.

For example, for the Chinese people the success of the 2008 Beijing Olympic Games was the culmination of long years of hope, an 11-year bid and a seven-year preparation! There was much to be savored, reflected upon and evaluated: there were tears and laughter. We can soak in the experience to draw new insights from the sentiments of others to make sense of our own emotions.

At the opening ceremony, when the national anthem of the People's Republic of China was being played in its grandeur, I felt an upsurge of emotions and sentiments, and instantly understood why I should relentlessly pursue dreams and excellence. I also realized that I should not be critical of the trivial things that come my way; but rather, with the end in mind, I should press forward without faltering to accomplish the task at hand.

Likewise, in the face of the huge natural disaster of the Sichuan earthquake of May 12, 2008, we not only read about the fragility of life, but also about how the people of China formed a cohesive force to support the relief efforts. We read about the most dependable strength of a people on the road to revival, which at the same time resonated with Lu Xun's words, "Only the souls of man are precious, and only through maximizing them can the nation of China truly progress." From the success of manned spaceship Shenzhou VII we once again hear the magnificent song of victory in the air. We read of the fulfillment of the dream for Chinese to walk in space, the culmination of the rigorous and meticulous approach to scientific work, of the composed attitudes and collaborative spirit, of the efforts to build an innovative country, and of the importance of all these for upgrading the nation's strength and accomplishing its development strategies.

On September 25, 2008, the whole world was watching China and looking to the universe, and there appeared the Descendents of the Dragon from deep space, leaving behind the footprints of the Chinese people. I was elated and joyously proud of China! However, in the face of boundless space and the advanced level of aerospace science and technology in developed countries, we realize that the future of China's space exploration has a long way to go.

In the experiences of the space program, the earthquake, the Olympic Games, the food safety and production safety incidents involving Sanlu milk powder and the collapse of a dam in Xiangfen county, the applause, flowers and celebrations are mixed with an awareness of the blood, tears and pain. The ancient saying goes, "Do not be surprised by affirmations and insults, for they are as common as flowers blossoming and wilting in the front yard; do not be affected by things that come or go, for they are as temporal as the clouds of the sky." We must strive not to blame others or belittle ourselves; and never be complacent or arrogant, but live firmly, steadily and peacefully.

There is much that we can learn, too, from the recent global financial tsunami that arose from the sub-prime mortgage crisis that spread from the United States to other parts of the world. With events such as these, we can get close to them, read and study them, integrating them into our storehouse of experience and wisdom.

HOW TO USE CLASSICS

The learning of classics is not for the purpose of putting up a good front, showing off knowledge, learning some nice words, generating some good comments, vocalizing some good ideas, or engaging in empty talk and futile writing. It is to upgrade the quality and ability of each of us, to make their guiding theories practicable, to solve practical problems, to promote work efficiency, to remodel work practices, and to create models which will themselves become classics of their kind. As Wu Jing commented long ago: "Applying is more difficult than knowing, while persevering is more challenging than applying."[12]

In 30 years of reform and opening up, the accountancy profession has achieved much in various arenas and is playing a more significant role in the process of socioeconomic development, leading to stronger international influence. But we should also be aware of our position at a new historical starting point. With outdated accounting information technology, imperfect mechanisms and systems for development, a shortage of skilled manpower, accounting regulatory concepts and tactics that are lagging behind, the Chinese accountancy profession is being held back from fully achieving sustainable development and emerging as a powerful international voice.

At the same time, in the face of diverse economic interests, values and objectives, and in the age of self-centered behavior, the quest for instant benefits from knowledge has seriously damaged the growth and development of the accounting elites, and challenged their academic isolation. While removing these barriers and constraints will not be an easy task, the knowledge crystallized in the classics can provide the theoretical basis and the source of strength to solve the problems we face. If we, the upcoming champions of accountancy, are to play a crucial role in this reform and development process, we must master the classics and put them to good use. To this end, I have some personal thoughts for you to reflect upon.

- **Learn to quote from the classics:** *The Book of the Later Han—Biography of Xun Shuang* advocates using the classics as the basis for argument: "The classics are where the righteous principles can be easily quoted from." This involves using recognized rationales, principles and methods to establish arguments to prove the real world, and grasping the laws of development in history to provide a clear guiding direction for future development. When performing tasks, reflecting on issues, and writing commentaries, we often provide a complete explanation or a more precise perspective and argument so as to better analyze the problem. In summary, a judicious use of quotes from the classics can be useful to enhance the scientific level, accuracy, credibility and persuasiveness of our thoughts and actions. In the classic texts, the language is often highly condensed, generalized and convincing, and when used appropriately, it will—to quote Mencius— "yield twice the returns for half the effort."

For thousands of years, the culture and traditions of the Eastern and Western worlds have nurtured countless classics and left us with boundless inspiration and space for creative development. Only by digesting, absorbing and reflecting on the core essence of these will we be able to use them wisely and well.

In this regard, Premier Wen Jiabao is a good example of how quoting from the classics can be used to good effect. At press conferences he is always full of confidence, with clear and flowing thoughts and a reservoir of good punch-lines while fielding questions. His answers are filled with famous quotes, stories and poems, and there are always new insights that are perfect for the occasion and refreshing to the mind.

For example, at the beginning of a press conference in 2006, Premier Wen said, "We must be sober-minded, cautious and prudent when times are good, as well as be mindful of potential problems and fully prepare for the worst." The words "sober-minded, cautious and prudent" were taken from *Jing River* from the Tang Dynasty, in which the saying goes, "There were no casualties for a long time at the dangerous Jing River for people were cautious; while accidents were aplenty at slow-flowing and rock-free rivers." His words "we must be mindful of potential problems and fully prepare for the worst" were taken from *Zuozhuan's Commentary on Spring and Autumn Annals—Eleven Years of Duke Xiang*. In his reply to questions on cross-strait relations, Premier Wen quoted a folk song from the *Historical Records—The Princes of Huainan and Hengshan*, "Even a foot of cloth can be stitched up, and a peck of millet can be ground," and he went on to amaze everybody by changing the last sentence of the folk song "How can two brothers not live in harmony?" to "How can two blood brothers not reconcile?" That was a sigh with a hope, advice with an inspiring challenge, which moved the hearts of the audience.

On other issues, Premier Wen quoted US economist and Nobel laureate in economics Theodore Schultz; and in response to a question on Sino-Indian relations, he cited a poem from the Indian scriptures, the *Upanishads*, which greatly enhanced the persuasiveness of his reply and brought thunderous applause. In late 2003, during an interview with the *Washington Post*, Premier Wen revealed, "Reading is my greatest and lifelong partner." Indeed, only a love for reading can cultivate such cultural wealth and ease with the classics.

The acumen to select the appropriate text and apply it to the needs of the moment is no easy task. Clearly, the ability is based on reading and studying the classics but it requires that we open our perspectives, break away from the common prejudices of the current times to include all the excellent cultural heritage and classical works.

Reading classics extensively places one in a better position to address audiences from different fields. When reading economics classics, we should expose ourselves to different schools of thought, as long as they reflect the laws of economic development. With regards to financial accounting theories, we should conduct extensive research to tap into the strengths of different theories. To stubbornly consider the works of a certain school of thought or particular style to be the only classic is to use classics in an inappropriate manner, and will greatly limit their impact.

The capacity to build our research on scientific, logical and firm foundations lies in our ability to identify and master previous classic literature.

• **Cultivate visual thinking:** Visual thinking is a way of thinking where judgments are made subjectively, using emotions rather than reasoning and analysis. It concentrates on the overall grasp rather than on the details, where knowledge is gained directly rather than through step-by-step logic. It is a form of intuitive, empirical thinking where new experiences are formed by gathering previous experiences and conclusions are drawn instantly and may be difficult to explain logically. Using visual thinking to observe objects and to analyze problems can bring about an epiphany, an upsurge of emotions and insights, which can then lead to the essence and heart of the matter.

Visual thinking has existed since ancient times, consciously or subconsciously, and is manifest in the vast historical and cultural classics. In the Chinese traditional view of the universe, man and everything else in the universe originated from Tao, and man is the center and measure of all things. Understanding of self leads to an understanding of the fundamentals of nature and the universe.

Confucianism's concept of man being "united with heaven and earth" and Taoism's "Heaven and I are created together, all creations are one with me" both reflect the characteristics of visual thinking. Wang Bi of the Wei-Jin Dynasty summed it up well:

> Words are generated from images, so one can ponder on words to understand images; images are generated from ideas, so one can ponder on images to understand ideas; ideas are made complete by images while images are made explicit by words; when a speaker grasps the image, the image will speak for itself; when one grasps the idea, he forgets the image.

Visual thinking is highly regarded in the classics of traditional Chinese literature and art, which emphasize that every image contains an idea and every idea stems from an image. For instance, Chinese painting emphasizes "the unity of form and spirit;" Chinese poetry emphasizes the "the integration of emotions and the surroundings;" Chinese music accentuates "the moving of feelings in the midst of sounds;" Chinese calligraphy focuses on "the expression of feelings by a writer," and so on. Imagery always stirs the soul, always commands, and always directs. Reading and quoting from the classics can help us to cultivate our own capacity for visual thinking.

Visual thinking regards "idea" (this usually refers to human consciousness, will, ideas, subjectivity) and "image" (objective matters, everything in the universe, and so on) as an integrated organism, where objects are personified to search for the law that governs the interaction between people and things. Literary, artistic and scientific innovation and the ability to discover and improve mathematics are inseparable from visual thinking (recently, a study by British scientists has shown that a person's mathematical ability is closely related to the numerical intuitive imagery in his early education). According to one well-known contemporary mathematician, "The mental imagery of the auditory model, sensory model and visual model is central to creative thinking."[13] Mozart used auditory imagery to hear the overall effect of a new symphony; French mathematician and philosopher Poincaré used sensory imagery to visualize the entire process of a mathematical proof; Einstein's creative thinking was produced by visual imagery, while the use of words to express creative thinking remains, he said, "the challenging task for the second stage."

Einstein was extremely fond of visual thinking. He once professed:

> I believe in inspiration and intuition . . . imagination is superior to knowledge, for knowledge is limited while imagination encompasses all there is in the world; it promotes progress and fuels the evolution of knowledge. Strictly speaking, imagination is an essential factor behind the success of any scientific research.

Just as visual thinking is pertinent to natural science and arts, accounting as an integral part of management also involves creative thinking through imagination and intuition. To become a true champion of accountancy, one who spearheads the accounting reform and development, one should focus on enhancing visual thinking. To exercise visual thinking, we need to unite "image" and "idea." The accounting profession often appears too rigid, too detailed or too conservative, reflecting little harmony between images and ideas. In the face of new opportunities and challenges, we need to break through the original mode of thinking, adopt new ideas, raise awareness, and strive to eliminate this restraint.

We must lay a solid foundation for visual thinking. Although visual thinking is incidental by nature, it is by no means empty thinking or random guesswork. It requires solid knowledge and extensive experience to continuously improve cognitive abilities. In this regard, we should learn from the artists. The poet Yu Guangzhong provided some insightful perspectives in his speech on "Experiencing Life through Art." He said that culture is the life and nature crafted by countless artists and writers through their sentiments and aesthetic sense, allowing us to experience life and observe nature through their eyes. Although much of life cannot be experienced personally by everyone, it can be vicariously lived through the experience of others. Some artworks based on legends or myths, which cannot be experienced directly, require us to use our knowledge, experience and imagination to interpret the beauty within. In other words, imagination can fill the gap created by the lack of experience. Finally, because creative works of art are based on knowledge, experience and imagination, and imagination is commonly recognized as the integration of knowledge and experience, imagination can be used to capture experience.

We should lay a solid foundation for cultivating visual thinking so that we can be like the poets and artists to sense the richness of the classics through direct or indirect experience, and to sense the reality of economic and social situations at those times. Only through the accumulation of knowledge and experience will we be able to face the objective world to attain enlightenment and inspiration.

We should continue to seek new breakthroughs in visual thinking, the formation of which is a gradual process. We should actively practice visual thinking in its formative stage, constantly adjusting our personal imagery structure by capturing an image and crystallizing an idea, forming an image based on an idea, or building an idea using an image, in order to achieve a perfect unity of image and idea. We should put aside details and allow generalization, abstraction and exaggeration, and extract the essence from the trivial, so as to comprehend the "Tao" behind the accounting reform and development and create an environment for self-development in the profession.

- **Extracting Principles for Leadership:** For the champions of accountancy, besides cultivating a correct outlook in life and correct values, it is also necessary to develop unique methods to carve out a career path. This not only involves skills but, more importantly, principles, which are embedded in the immortal classics left behind by our predecessors.

Classics were not meant to be rigid dogma; rather, with in-depth reading and repeated meditation, it is possible to understand the implicit philosophy, wisdom and methodology, and to personalize these as the "internal mechanism" of our leadership—in temperament, bearing, daily living and behavior, putting them into practice in dealing with complex issues and leading the team. There is much to be said on the topic of extracting principles for leadership from the classics, but I would like to use the following phrase from Sun Tzu's *The Art of War* as the basis of our discussion: "The commander stands for the virtues of wisdom, sincerity, benevolence, courage and strictness."

As one writer put it: "Wisdom determines vision, vision determines decisions, decisions determine fate, and fate determines the future."[14] Only wise people can lead in the accountancy profession. We can find wisdom in the classics and from the characters in the classics. For example, from Zhuge Liang's *Longzhong Plan*, the tripartite confrontation ultimately arose from Liu Bei's decisions and directions, guided by an analysis of the vantage point of the overall situation and strategic perspectives in the situation at that time. The wisdom here lay in the correct analysis and grasp of the situation. Similar wisdom was on display too when the Japanese invaded China in 1937. The great Mao Zedong had a clear grasp of what was required and his thesis that "the war against Japan can only be a protracted one" proved to be correct. In December 1948, when the war of liberation was in full swing, the Nationalist government in Nanjing requested peace talks, hoping to divide China between the two administrations. Mao remembered Chu-Han's "Division Agreement" mentioned in the *Historical Records*, sized up the situation, and decisively remarked, "It is easy to pursue the tottering foe with power to spare, but we must not ape the conqueror seeking idle fame."[15]

In addition, we must determine, borrow and apply the potential within the wisdom of the classics. Sun Tzu says, "The energy of good fighting men is like the momentum of a round stone rolling down a mountain thousands of feet high—that is potential." This is the wisdom of using "potential." At present, China's socioeconomic development is passing through an important period of deepening reform and expansion, and there will definitely be greater development in the accountancy profession. It is a worthy task for every leader to repeatedly cogitate on how to analyze and grasp situations, and on how to borrow and use the available potential.

Second, we must assert authority based on "sincerity." In *The Art of War*, the meaning of "sincerity" is to reward and punish impartially, and to be honest without taking advantage of others to ensure that the team is combat-effective. The philosopher Han Feizi[16] said, "When there is impartiality in rewarding and punishing, people are prepared to face challenges." In other words, in order for people to trust, obey and follow you, you need to be honest and not take advantage of others. With that, your team will have few reasons to fail. Even today, the classic case of Zhuge Liang's tearful execution of Ma Su is still worth savoring.[17]

Shuo Wen Jie Zi[18] tells us that the Chinese word for "benevolence" is made up of two people loving each other. In *The Analects of Confucius*, Confucius interpreted it as "love for people." If we have a benevolent heart, people with lofty ideals will gather around us to help us achieve success. Sun Tzu said, "Treat your soldiers as your children, and they will follow you into the deepest valleys; look upon them as your own beloved sons, and they will stand by you even unto death." This is the force of benevolence!

"Enthusiasm is to be shown only to the virtuous, and plans for the country are only to be shared with the learned. Few are those who can neglect the virtuous and slight the learned, and still maintain the existence of their countries."[19] In the absence of virtuous and learned people, emergencies will become overwhelming, and there will be no one with whom to plan national affairs. No country has ever attained long-term stability by neglecting the learned and ignoring the talented. To attract talent through benevolence requires tolerance and a breadth of vision to consider "everyone from across the world my brother"[20] and to comprehend that "a phoenix attracts a hundred birds."[21] A colony of bees will follow their queen to the east and west; geese fly with their leader to the north and south; when the rooster crows, a hundred chickens sing with him; when a horse starts running, a thousand horses gallop alongside. If we wish to attract "a hundred birds," we must first attract "the phoenix." The Chinese traditional culture and classics place special emphasis on the role of "benevolence," as reflected in *The Analects of Confucius*. By grasping the true meaning of "benevolence," and effectively putting it into practice, hearts can be united and every talented accounting leader can achieve success in his career.

Zhuge Liang in his *Xin Shu* said, "Diligently attracting a hero's heart is essential in the army." Courage has always been a key quality in elite personnel. The "courage" mentioned in *The Art of War* is a courage of the spirit, courage based on strategy, and not everyday courage. This kind of courage is needed to lead a team well, and to spearhead the trends in the profession. It is necessary for firm decision-making at crucial moments, and to face the consequences of the decision. This kind of courage is not reckless; it is based on planning. The principles in the classics lay the groundwork for establishing sound practice or research into academic theories, and for grasping the essence of things in the face of today's complex and rapidly changing circumstances.

In practice, it takes a qualitative leap to discover the nature of things from appearances, something which people who are unable to grasp principles find difficult to do. A short story from *Guanzi* illustrates this point: One day, Duke Han of Qi said to Minister Guan Zhong, "A few days ago, I was at the hunting ground, when suddenly a fierce tiger jumped out, and after exchanging a few glances with the horse I was riding, quietly slipped away. Don't you find it strange?" Minister Guan Zhong replied, "According to legend, there was a tiger-eating beast, known as the Jun, which bore a deep resemblance to a horse. Was the sun behind your Highness at that time?" The Duke said, "Yes, it was!" Guan Zhong said, "As the tiger was looking into the sun, the horse looked like Jun, which is why the tiger backed away in fear." This story, though brief, pointed out a profound truth. Appearance can be deceptive but if we are able to look beyond to study and grasp the essence, we will become wise in the long run and shine in our leadership.

Strict discipline is always essential to maintain regular order and sustainable development in any organization. Without it, an organization or team would be like scattered sand, fighting their own battles and losing their way. Early records of this can be found in China's traditional history, culture and classics. The *Book of History* says, "There was a great battle at Kan, and the king had called together six nobles. The king said, 'You who obey my orders, shall be rewarded before my ancestors; and you who disobey my orders, shall be put to death . . . together with your children.'"

US General George Patton, a classic military character and a prominent figure in the Second World War, also knew the importance of discipline. He once said: "Discipline is an important factor for maintaining the combat effectiveness of troops, and also a basic safeguard to maximize the potential of the soldiers. Therefore, discipline should be deep-rooted, and it has to be stronger than the intensity of war and the terrible nature of death." There was no room for individualism in the military, he cautioned; only discipline—which was an important reason for his success.

The Communist Party of China, which has led the Chinese people to victory time and again, also uses iron discipline as protection. In the Jinggangshan period, the great man Mao Zedong personally scripted and issued a classic book of discipline. Entitled *Three Main Rules of Discipline and Eight Points for Attention*, it is still shining the light of wisdom on us to this day. By absorbing the words and actions of such characters and using them to manage a team well, we will experience success.

The words of Xunzi in his letter *Quanxue* (Encourage Learning) are worth bearing in mind at all times:

> Standing high to beckon does not lengthen the arm, but catches the attention of those far away; calling in the direction of the wind does not increase the volume, but is heard by many; riding a horse does not make one a better runner, but brings one through a thousand miles; riding a boat does not make one a swimmer, but brings one through rivers. A gentleman may not be superior to others, but he is wise in using things around him.

A high-talented accountant should excel in copying the lessons contained in the classics to enhance his skills, strengthen his principles and plant within his heart the good seed of their true essence. By doing so, he will equip himself to lead the development of the profession and contribute to the socioeconomic development of the nation.

- **Determination to create a classic:** The great thing about the classic texts that have shaped our world today is the fact that they have provided a basis for great thinkers and leaders of subsequent generations to build upon and remodel their central ideas in line with new knowledge and the needs of the time. Thus, the process of development and improvement goes on from generation to generation. By studying the classics, the leading accounting talent is expected to develop and improve on the classics, and on the basis of that, to create new classics.

For example, the ancient Greek philosopher Aristotle was an outstanding student of Plato and was the first to distinguish philosophy from the other sciences of his day. He created disciplines such as logic, ethics, political science and biology. Works such as *Physics*, *On the Heavens*, *Meteorology*, *Politics*, *Rhetoric* and so on have been passed down through the centuries and have left an indelible mark on the development of Western culture.

Another familiar example is the sixteenth-century astronomer and mathematician Nicolaus Copernicus, whose classic work *On the Revolutions of the Celestial Spheres* changed age-old thinking and beliefs about the workings of the universe and began a scientific revolution in his day. His work was taken further by the Italian atheist and scholar Giordano Bruno, who was burned to death for challenging the established beliefs of his day.

The great man Mao Zedong is another classic example of the dynamic application and remodeling of accepted wisdom to forge something new and more applicable for the specific circumstances of a particular time and place. Having studied, absorbed and understood the classic Marxist texts, he took and developed their legacy in a different direction by applying them to the particular realities of China's revolution. Revolutionary Maoist thought had, and continues to have, a significant influence on both China and the wider world.

Pan Xulun, the eminent accountant, obtained a doctorate in the United States in his early years, founded the Pan Xulun Accounting Firm in 1927, and in 1928 founded Lixin Accounting School, China's first school of accounting. From his practice, Pan understood the importance of gaining trust from the community, and adopted the essence of "a nation stands on the trust of its people" from *The Analects of Confucius*. Lixin's code of conduct—"Integrity in building ambition, integrity in preserving oneself, integrity in dealings, integrity in treating others—always build integrity, and you will succeed"— became highly regarded and set the tone for the accounting profession in China.

Such examples are worthy of our attention. Certain PhD training institutes in China attach great importance to their students' mastery of classic literature. The students are often required to read dozens of classic works, Chinese and foreign, in their assignments to clarify the context in order to grasp the essence. In my opinion, this is a very good style of training and education.

In seeking to emulate our predecessors, we should have a correct understanding of history and of the times, and grasp the laws of social and accounting development to set a clear research direction. Today, we, the leading talents in the accountancy profession, have advantages that were not available to our predecessors. The development of the various disciplines of study, the progress in research methods, the closeness and frequent communication in the international community, and the openness of the internet have enabled us to recognize and grasp the laws of development more easily, using them to serve the times and society. The leading talents in the accountancy profession, theoreticians and practitioners alike, can only become great accountants and trendsetters in the modern era by taking the pulse of the times and capitalizing on society's needs and the laws of development.

We must learn from diverse sources. It is necessary to absorb and store knowledge and wisdom in order to establish a broader view of accounting. In order to establish practical development, technology upgrades and international cooperation that are part of the modern world, we must break out of the cocoon of common prejudices by taking into consideration accounting theories, methods and results from modern, ancient, domestic and foreign sources. Only by having an eager, proactive and persevering spirit to explore the wisdom of the world can we establish the greatness of accounting in China and become a great master of modern accounting.

We must consciously assume responsibilities. In a recent essay on "the commitment to academic research," Professor Qian Liqun set out his belief that while engaging in academic research it is essential to make "academia one's life, having a self-sustaining existence consisting of academia without the need for anything else; where academia itself is the meaning and value of life." If we are to achieve our goals for the accounting profession, it is necessary to have such a group of scholars who embrace academic accounting research as their life, such that reading, thinking, researching and creating become their means of existence, permeating into their daily lives and bringing them into the long-lasting state of joy that the research brings. The real masters of accounting can only come into being as these unique groups continue to grow in strength.

We must be bold to innovate. We must nurture innovative potential and master innovative ways. Innovation is the key to national progress. At an opportune time for major developments in the accountancy profession, the key to successful innovation and breakthroughs lies in the ability of individuals to master innovative ways and put them to good use. In this regard, the first key is to have sharp discernment. Discernment is the ability to perceive, sense and analyze knowledge, emotions and behavior and their interrelationships, and to capture and discover the desired things such as knowledge and truth. This requires us to be diligent in thinking, skilled at observation, while maintaining a deep understanding and grasp of financial accounting issues in the socioeconomic life of the nation.

The second key to unleash innovative potential is to have a rich imagination. Imagination is the capability to fit pieces of information into a larger, neutral picture of integrated visual images that shows their interrelationships. In making classics for accounting, we have to give full play to imagination, and focus on performing "nuclear reaction" on the reality of socioeconomic life.

With regard to innovative potential, the third key is to be decisive. Decisiveness is the ability of a person to make judgments and timely decisions. A person who hesitates to assume responsibility, to back his ideas and to take risks, and who fails to have an opinion of his own, is bound to fail in any business. Decisiveness is an important factor for innovation.

After watching the Beijing Olympic Games, I believe that the fourth key to maximize the innovative potential is to have a "champion mentality." Great athletes, artists, scientists and even politicians, though of different fields, all display this mentality. Champions always pursue their dreams and are willing to give up worldly pleasures to work diligently and tirelessly; they have an unyielding spirit. Though they may often fail, they refuse to be defeated by failure and will always stand up stronger than before. Champions have the courage to run ahead of the pack; they will not follow the beaten track, but will take the road less traveled to achieve breakthroughs and create a new world altogether.

The fifth key is to have superb language proficiency, of which I have spoken many times.

While on the subject of innovation, my contact with various university deans and professors in recent years have revealed their genuine concerns regarding the serious stagnation of national accounting education. Because of this, during the first half of the first semester in our academic classes, we paid particular attention to the study of international accounting research methods. This is a very important point. My hope is for every highly-talented accountant in the profession to strengthen his innovative potential through learning the classic texts to lay a solid foundation for innovation and the making of future classics.

We must live above fame and fortune, get away from the voices of the world. We must withstand temptations and loneliness, continually nurture and retain our spiritual heritage, allow ourselves to be incubators for the classics and trailblazers on the paths less traveled and for the methods less explored. On this point, famous lines from Wang Guowei's *Human Words and Language* come to mind:

> The great achievers and gurus of all time must pass through three realms to achieve success. The first realm says, "As the green trees withered in the autumn wind of last evening, I went up to the tower alone, and overlooked a road reaching the skyline." The second realm says, "No regrets if my clothes become loose, if I become haggard for my lady who has disappeared." The third realm says, "I have searched a thousand times to no avail, but all of a sudden as I turn around, I saw her under the dimmed lights."

Only by passing through the exploration and hardship of the first two realms will we, as leading champions of accountancy, reach the "third realm," experiencing new discoveries, new inspirations, new creations, and hence attaining the highest level of accounting achievements.

Accounting classics are the embodiment of the development of the accountancy profession in their time. Their impact is far greater than hundreds of commonplace literary products. Though existing research and practices are highly dynamic, recognized cornerstone works which can be passed down to future generations are still scarce. The current and continuing growth in theoretical research and practice signals that there will be a corresponding increase in both the quantity and quality of written materials from which will emerge more classics. As leading talents in the accountancy profession, we should be committed to using existing classics to remodel and create new accounting classics.

"Although Zhou was an ancient state, it had a reformed mission. In the midst of abundance, the old can be viewed through new lenses."[22] China is currently in an important period, with imminent development opportunities and challenges. My hope is that we live up to the expectations of the times, rise up to the call of our leaders, and understand, develop, create and apply work that will become the classics of our time. With our eyes set on transforming the accountancy profession into a "classic" profession, let's play our part in this great journey of development and reform, displaying true heroism and making history for the Chinese nation.

ENDNOTES

1 Based on a speech given at the Inaugural Ceremony of the Training Program of National (Prospective) Leading Accountancy Talents, October 25, 2008.

2 Lin Yutang (1895–1976) is a famous Chinese writer, philosopher and translator. He wrote more than 35 books and his compilations and translations of classic Chinese texts into English were bestsellers in the West. After 1928, he lived mainly in the United States.

3 The relationship between *yin* and *yang* is often described in terms of sunlight playing over a mountain and in the valley. *Yin* (literally the "shady place" or "north slope") is the dark area occluded by the mountain's bulk, while *yang* (literally the "sunny place" or "south slope") is the brightly lit portion. As the sun moves across the sky, *yin* and *yang* gradually trade places with each other, revealing what was obscured and obscuring what was revealed. *Yin* is usually characterized as slow, soft, insubstantial, diffuse, cold, wet, and tranquil. It is generally associated with the feminine, birth and generation, and with the night. *Yang*, by contrast, is characterized as hard, fast, solid, dry, focused, hot, and aggressive. It is associated with masculinity and daytime.

4 This refers to the method developed by the mathematician Hua Luogeng. Guided by the mathematical principles, it aims to find the optimum solution in manufacturing and scientific experiments with the minimum possible tests.

5 From a well-known poem by Du Fu (712–770), a prominent Chinese poet of the Tang Dynasty.

6 Li Dazhao (1888–1927) was a professor of history and librarian at Peking University, one of the founders of the Chinese Communist Party. He was the first important Chinese intellectual to support the Bolshevik Revolution in Russia.

7 Poem by Xin Qiji (1140–1207), a famous poet of Southern Song Dynasty.

8 These words are from the book *Muo Shu* (Touch the book) by Feng Jicai (1942–) and published in 1993 by Shanxi People Press.

9 In this work, Qu Yuan (340–278BC) criticized the fatuity of the King of Chu. However, his suggestions were not adopted by the King. Qu Yuan committed suicide by drowning himself in the Miluo River.

10 Quoted from Benedetto Croce (1866–1952), an Italian critic, idealist philosopher, and occasional politician.

11 For a full list, see the Appendix.

12 In *Essentials of Politics during Zhen Guan's Reign—Being Careful with the Outcome* (Tang Dynasty).

13 Miller, I. 1984, *Imagery in Scientific Thought: Creating 20th-Century Physics*, Birkhauser Boston Inc.

14 From a review of Peter F. Drucker's book *The Effective Executive* by Zhan Wenming, a former student of Drucker's.

15 This relates to a story from around 200BC involving two heroes—Liu Bang and Xiang Yu. Liu Bang's army was beaten by Xiang Yu's, but Xiang Yu showed mercy to his former friend. Later, however, Liu Bang killed Xiang Yu. Mao Zedong wrote these words towards the end of the war against Chiang Kai-shek to show that he would not imitate Xiang Yu.

16 Han Feizi (281–233 BC), a philosopher, thinker, politician and writer in the Warring States Period.

17 Ma Su, a famous general, once disregarded the orders of his leader, Zhuge Liang, which led to the destruction of Zhuge's army. In order to punish him and to emphasize the impartiality of his regulations, Zhuge Liang had Ma Su executed, though with great regret.

18 *Shuo Wen Jie Zi*, literally "Explaining Simple and Analyzing Compound Characters," was an early second-century dictionary from the Han Dynasty compiled by Xu Shen (58–147).

19 From *Mo Zi*, a compilation of the thoughts of the philosopher Mo Zi (468–376BC).

20 From Zi Xia, a disciple of Confucius.

21 This is a Chinese proverb. The phoenix is an imaginary bird which, according to legend, had once been an ordinary bird. It was very diligent, picking up and saving all the grain that the other birds left. One year a massive drought left no food for birds and the phoenix benevolently offered all the grain it had saved to the other birds. The birds were very grateful; each gave the phoenix one of its most beautiful feathers and respected the phoenix as their king. Where there was a phoenix, many birds were attracted.

22 From the *Book of Poetry* (Western Zhou 1046–771BC) and quoted by Chinese premier Wen Jiabao at a press conference to indicate that China, an old country with a long history, has a mission to reform and China will continue to reform and bring in new views to co-exist with the old.

APPENDIX

Politics and Natural Sciences:

Selected Works of Mao Zedong, Selected Works of Deng Xiaoping, Selected Works of Jiang Zemin, Reading of Scientific Outlook on Development, Zhenguan Administration (by Wu Jing), *Sixteen Policies* (by Zhuge Liang), *The Prince* (by Machiavelli), *Nine-Chapter Arithmetic, A Series of Books on Chinese Mathematics History* (by Wu Wenjun et al.), *Mathematical Principles of Natural Philosophy* (by Isaac Newton), *A Brief History of Science* (by William Cecil Dampier) and *A Brief History of Time* (by Stephen Hawking).

Humanities:

The **History and Philosophy** section includes *The Book of Changes, Laotze, The Analects of Confucius, Mencius, Chuang Tzu, The Book of History, Intrigues of the Warring States, Zi Zhi Tong Jian, A Brief History of Chinese Philosophy* (by Fung Yu-lan), *Chinese Brief History* (by Bo Yang), *The Bible, Meditations* (by Marcus Aurelius), *The Theory of Moral Sentiments* (by Adam Smith), *Dialogues* (by Plato), *Les Pensées* (by Blaise Pascal), *A History of Western Philosophy* (by Bertrand Russell), *The Spirit of the Laws* (by Charles de Montesquieu), *Philosophy Notes* (by Vladimir Lenin), *On Protracted War*.

The **Literature and Arts section** includes *The Book of Songs, The Song of the South, Best of Classical Prose, The Classic of Mountains and Rivers, Three Hundred Poems of Tang Dynasty, Note and Commentary on Three Hundred Ci Poetry of the Song Dynasty, A Dream of Red Mansions, Complete Works of Lu Xun, Fortress Besieged* (by Qian Zhongshu), *Dialogue As A Style* (by Plato), *Collected Works of Shakespeare, How the Steel Was Tempered* (by Nikolai Ostrovsky), *War and Peace* (by Leo Tolstoy), *The Divine*

Comedy (by Dante), *Jean-Christophe* (by Romain Rolland), *The Old Man and the Sea* (by Ernest Hemingway), *One Hundred Years of Solitude* (by Gabriel Garcia Marquez), and Rabindranath Tagore's *Gitanjali* and *Stray Birds*.

Economics:

Das Kapital (by Karl Marx), *Theory of Taxation* (by William Petty), *On the Nature of Wealth, Money and Tax* (by Pierre Le Pesant de Boisguillebert), *Principles of Political Economy and Taxation* (by David Ricardo), *The Wealth of Nations* (Adam Smith), *An Essay on the Principle of Population* (by Robert Malthus), *New Principles of Political Economy* (by Simonde de Sismondi), *The National System of Political Economy* (by Friedrich List), *The Origins of Family, Private Ownership and Country* (by Friedrich Engels), *Principles of Economics* (by Alfred Marshall), *The Distribution of Wealth* (by John Bates Clark), *The Theory of Economic Development* (by Joseph Schumpeter), *Welfare Economics* (by Arthur Cecil Pigou), *Economics of Imperfect Competition* (by Joan Robinson), *The General Theory of Employment, Interest and Money* (by John Maynard Keynes), *Value and Capital* (by John Richard Hicks), *Economics* (by Paul A. Samuelson, *et al.*), *Capitalism and Freedom* (by Milton Friedman), *Public Choice Theory* (by James McGill Buchanan), *Economics* (by Joseph E. Stiglitz), *The Economics of Taxation* (by Bernard Salanie), *Principles of Finance* (by Richard Abel Musgrave), *Public Finance: A Contemporary Application of Theory to Policy* (by David N. Hyman), *Principles of Economics* (by Greg Mankiw), *Selected Works on Economics of Robert Mundell*, *Morgan Financial Group* (by Ron Chernow), *Beating the Street* (by Peter Lynch), *Value at Risk* (by Philippe Jorion), *Game Theory: Analysis of Conflict* (by Roger B. Myerson), *The World Is Flat* (by Thomas L. Friedman).

Management:

The Principles of Scientific Management (by Frederick Winslow Taylor), *Theories on Social and Economic Organizations* (by Max Weber), *The Functions of the Executive* (by Chester Irving Barnard), *The New Science of Management Decision* (by Herbert Alexander Simon), *New Patterns of Management* (by Rensis Likert), *Marketing Management* (by Philip Kotler), *Criteria of Organizational Effectiveness* (by Stanley E. Seashore), *Organization and Management: A*

System and Contingency Approach (by Fremont E. Kast *et al.*), *Jack: Straight from the Gut* (by Jack Welch), *Competitive Strategy* (by Michael Porter), *Theory Z* (by William Ouchi), *The General Managers* (by John P. Kotter), *In Search of Excellence* (by Tom Peters), *Leaders: The Strategies for Taking Charge* (by Warren G. Bennis), *Re-engineering* (by Michael Hammer), *Internal Control—Integrated Framework* and *Enterprise Risk Management—Integrated Framework* (by Committee of Sponsoring Organizations of the Treadway Commission).

Accounting and Auditing:

Kwong Sui Accounting Statements (by Liu Yueyun, the chief official of feudal Chinese Ministry of Revenue in Qing Dynasty), *Lixin Accounting Series* (established by Pan Xulun), *Good Will and Other Intangible Assets* (by Yang Rumei), *Principles of Accounting* (by Yang Jiwan, Lou Erxing, Ge Jiashu, Zhao Yumin and Wu Cheng), *Theoretical Structure of Accounting* (by A.C. Littleton), *An Introduction to Corporate Accounting Standards* (by William Andrew Paton and A.C. Littleton), *Handbook of Modern Accounting* (by Sidney Davidson), *Accounting Theory* (by Eldon S. Hendriksen), *History of Accounting* (by Guo Daoyang), *A History of Accounting Thought* (by Michael Chatfield), *Positive Accounting Theory* (by Ross L. Watts), *Advanced Management Accounting* (by Robert S. Kaplan), *Financial Accounting Conceptual Framework* (by Financial Accounting Standards Board), *Montgomery's Auditing* (by Montgomery) and *Brink's Modern Internal Accounting* (by Robert R. Moeller and Herbert N. Witt).

INDEX